US Army Yearbook 2025

CONTENTS

ABOVE: A soldier from the 41st Infantry BCT, Oregon National Guard, lays down covering fire for a breaching team during an exercise at Fort Johnson Louisiana. (US ARMY)

LEFT: A soldier pretending to be an enemy prepares to throw a grenade simulator at two soldiers of the 173rd Airborne Brigade during Exercise Saber Junction 24 in Hohenfels, Germany. (US ARMY)

MAIN COVER IMAGE: An automatic rifleman exits a Stryker Dragoon fighting vehicle during Exercise Eagle Partner 24. (US ARMY)

ISBN: 978 1 83632 055 5
Editor: Chris Miskimon
Senior editor, specials: Roger Mortimer
Email: roger.mortimer@keypublishing.com
Cover Design: Steve Donovan
Design: SJmagic DESIGN SERVICES, India
Advertising Sales Manager: Sam Clark
Email: sam.clark@keypublishing.com
Tel: 01780 755131
Advertising Production: Becky Antoniades
Email: Rebecca.antoniades@keypublishing.com

SUBSCRIPTION/MAIL ORDER
Key Publishing Ltd, PO Box 300, Stamford, Lincs, PE9 1NA
Tel: 01780 480404
Subscriptions email: subs@keypublishing.com
Mail Order email: orders@keypublishing.com
Website: www.keypublishing.com/shop

PUBLISHING
Group CEO and Publisher: Adrian Cox

Published by
Key Publishing Ltd, PO Box 100, Stamford, Lincs, PE9 1XQ

Tel: 01780 755131
Website: www.keypublishing.com

PRINTING
Precision Colour Printing Ltd, Haldane, Halesfield 1, Telford, Shropshire. TF7 4QQ

DISTRIBUTION
Seymour Distribution Ltd, 2 Poultry Avenue, London, EC1A 9PU
Enquiries Line: 02074 294000.

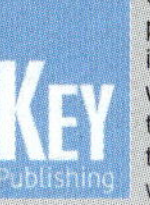

Welcome

Welcome to the third edition of the US Army Yearbook. This annual publication looks at the US Army with a focus on the past year's developments, exercises and real-world operations. It also provides general background information to help the reader better understand how the US Army is organised and equipped. We will look at some of the service's formative past operations and conflicts, revealing how it got to its present state. Perhaps most importantly, the reader will see what the US Army is doing to prepare for the next conflict.

Our major theme this year is on the US Army's efforts to modernise not only its weapons and equipment, but its units and personnel. The army has closely followed the changes seen worldwide in various conflicts, including the ongoing war in Ukraine and fighting in several places in the Middle East. Both conflicts are a mix of longstanding tactical concepts with new technologies used in new and original ways. The fighting in the Middle East is a mix of new developments in the region combined with the continuation of decades-long problems stemming from the War on Terror period and back to the Cold War. The army's efforts to prepare for any possible war is called 'Transformation in Contact.'

These conflicts show the evolving nature of tactics and weapons applied to age-old concepts such as attack, defence, movement, and manoeuvre. Unmanned Aerial Systems (UAS) have been around for decades but are seeing new methods of employment and widespread proliferation, mostly in small, inexpensive platforms. Autonomous and remotely controlled ground systems are also becoming common. Perhaps most importantly, UAS and other new technologies are enabling fast cycles of reconnaissance, targeting and attack. The army is concerned about survivability in such a battlefield environment.

In this edition we will look at some of the technologies, plans and exercises the army is conducting. It is experimenting on how to stay flexible and ready to fight on short notice. It also realises it might need to adopt new weapons and technologies very quickly, getting an initial ability and improving it on the battlefield in real time.

This preparation is happening while the army is actively involved in training, exercises and actual combat operations around the world. The reader is invited to take note of how many photograph captions have the words 'undisclosed location' in them. This is a hint at how heavily involved the US Army currently is in Middle Eastern conflicts, both in combat and deterrence missions. Note that almost all images in this edition are less than one year old from time of publishing.

The US Army has 20 divisions, each of two to four brigade combat teams (BCTs). This year we look at all of them with detailed information on each unit's order of battle, down to each combat battalion's nickname if known. The US Army's Special Force's units get a closer look as well. Although these units prefer to operate covertly, there is a lot of attention given them and a lot of information put out about them and their operations. Much of it is incorrect, so we lay out the basic facts about the Rangers, the Green Berets and the Combat Applications Group, also known as Delta Force. The four historical operations in this edition are all about rescue operations conducted by Special Operations forces; some ended well, others did not, but they show the evolution of US Army capabilities in that realm.

The two reserve components of the army, the National Guard and Army Reserve, also receive extra coverage. The US Army cannot fight effectively in a major conflict without these two forces. The National Guard in particular has some uniquely American details in its makeup and we present them to the reader.

Our yearbook ends with our best educated guesses at how the army fits into four contingency scenarios for conflicts which could occur in the near future. A war involving the US in any of these global hotspots would heavily involve the US Army, even possible Pacific operations which many think would be the province of the US Navy and US Air Force. The army brings vital abilities to any fight.

There is a general concern in the US military that a major conflict may occur in the next five to ten years. Much of what you might see in media about the risk of war in the near future is simple punditry or even outright paranoia. However, some senior military officers are concerned that given the current rise in political instability around the globe, the chance of a conflict is growing higher.

Darker predictions compare the current environment to 1938, but army leaders have a more sober outlook. They realise there are too many external variables to make any prediction wholly certain. These leaders also know that proper preparation can equal deterrence so that war never starts. Transformation in Contact shows that if any conflict does break out, the army intends to be ready to fight and win.

Christopher Miskimon
Major, Field Artillery, USA (Ret.)
Editor

The US Army Today

Transformation and preparation equal deterrence

RIGHT: A paratrooper of the 82nd Airborne Division disembarks from a CH47 Chinook helicopter during a mission at an undisclosed location in Syria. (US ARMY)

BELOW: US Army Chief of Staff General Randy George places a Legion of Merit award on UK Chief of the General Staff General Sir Patrick Sanders and Australian Chief of Army Lieutenant General Simon Stuart during a ceremony at Fort Myers, Virginia. (US ARMY)

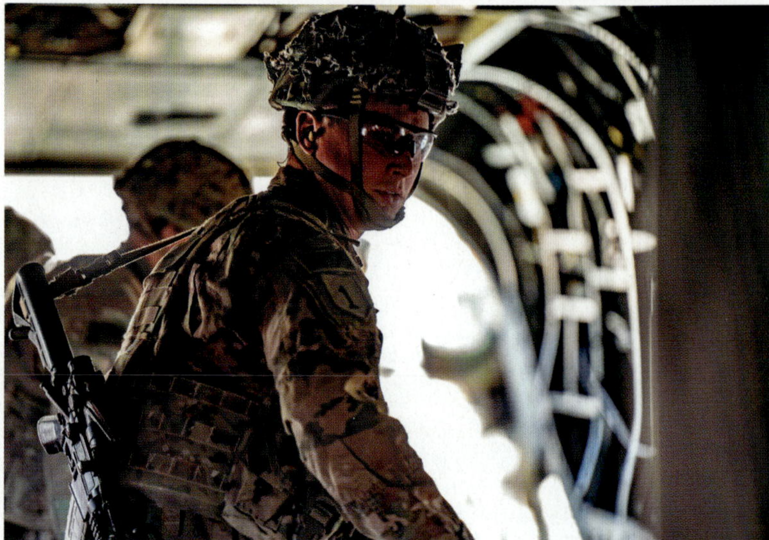

The US Army wants to be so well-prepared for the next war that it never has to fight it. Ongoing conflicts in Ukraine and the Middle East are demonstrating new warfighting technologies and concepts which point towards the nature of that next war. However, the pace of technological change is currently so fast that even the most successful new devices, currently dominating the battlefield, may be obsolete within a year or two. The army must not only keep pace with evolving technology but also employ it effectively.

This means the army must develop new acquisition methods to get new technologies and equipment into soldiers hands quickly. The days of years-long development programmes for every new system are ending; instead, the army wants to get a functional capability into the hands of its soldiers, let them test it in exercises and actual operations, then make changes and improvements in

service. If the army and US military as a whole can successfully develop this rapid acquisition process, it will be able to rapidly improve battlefield effectiveness even as a conflict is ongoing.

Achieving this goal may not be as hard as it seems. Almost all of the new technologies are in areas such as targeting, command and control and Intelligence, Surveillance and Reconnaissance (ISR). Many large

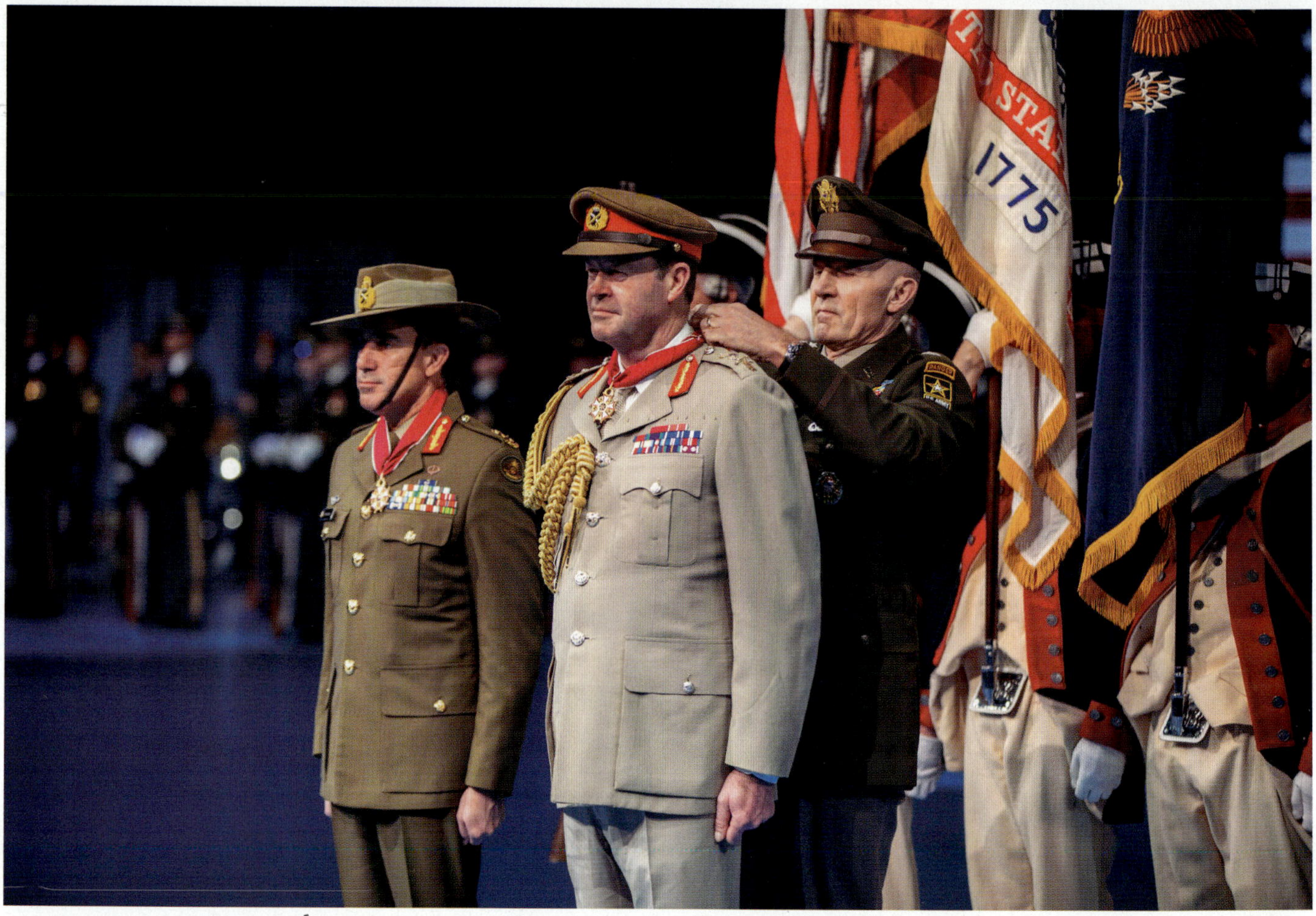

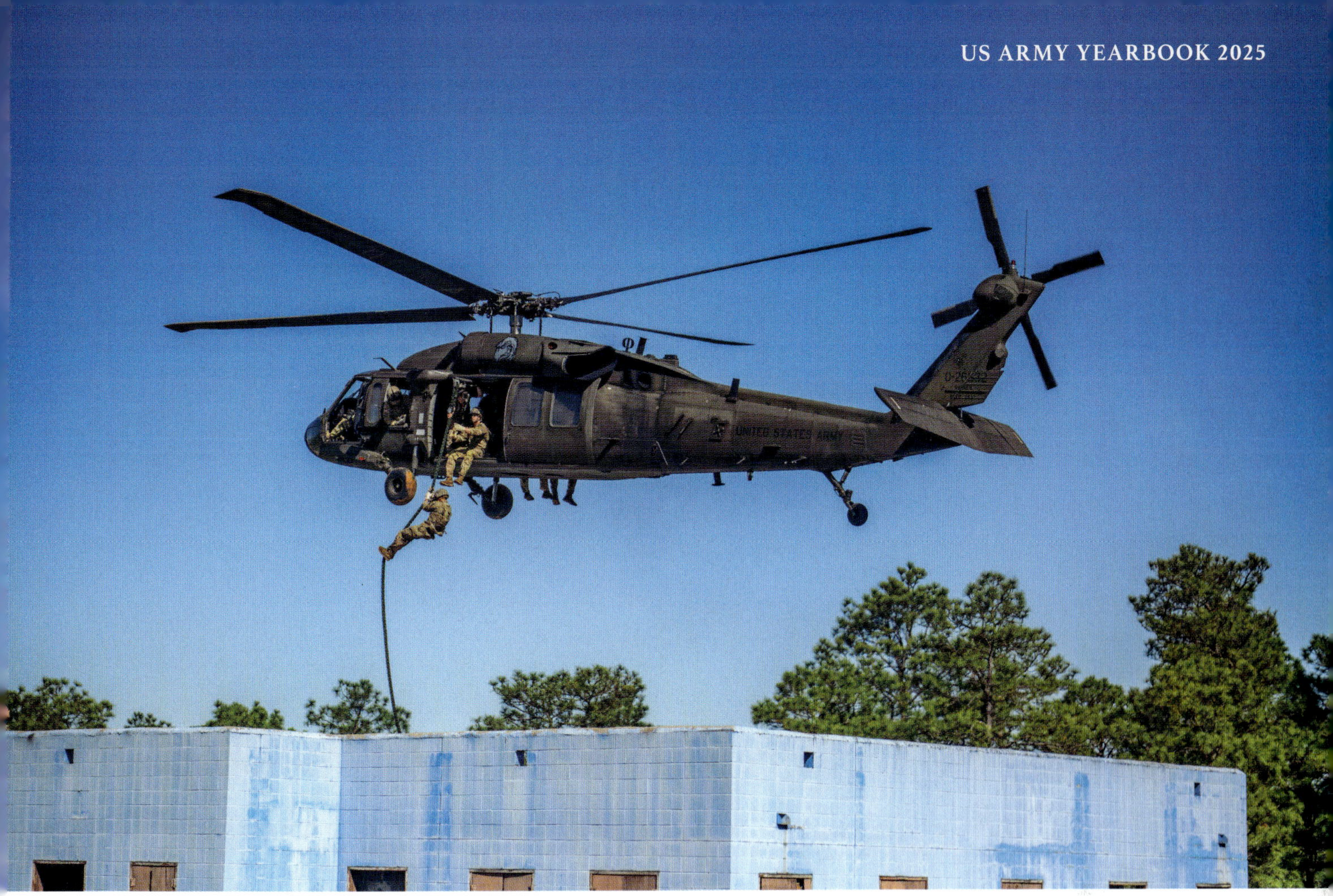

systems have not changed much in decades; rather the systems used to employ them have advanced radically. For example, basic cannons, mortars, machine guns and other weapons have changed little in decades, while the systems used to locate their targets and quickly develop fire plans to strike them have advanced dramatically.

These systems and equipment are generally electronic/digital in nature, which actually can allow easier replacement and upgrade. Furthering our example, a reader might be looking at this publication on a mobile device of some kind. That device is durable, probably serving several years or more, but it must be periodically upgraded to increase its capabilities and keep it secure. The army must develop ways to do the same thing, large-scale, across the force without costly years-long development programmes. Army Chief of Staff General Randy George is confident the US Army can do so, saying in a recent speech: "The tech we will infuse in our formations are not years away, they are available now."

Sense, Strike and Survive: This term from a 2024 Army War College annual estimate acknowledges the growing battlefield challenge of finding the enemy, hitting them, and then avoiding or hardening against their counterstrike. Toward this end the army is focusing on targeting, offensive capabilities, and survivability. At the army level, there are four new types of units being created:

Multi-Domain Task Force: A brigade-sized combination of long-range artillery, air defence, signals, and electronic warfare units to be employed at the theater level. These units have been under development for several years and the US Army intends to raise five such units to their full authorised strength.

Indirect Fire Protection Capability (IFPC) Battalions: These units provide short to medium range defence against UAS, missiles, artillery, and mortars. The US Army wants to field four more battalions in addition to the five already planned.

Counter-Small Unmanned Aerial Systems (C-sUAS) Batteries: The US Army wants nine batteries of this new unit type, which will be incorporated into IFPC and division-level air defence battalions to bolster defence against small UAS.

Maneuver Short-Range Air Defense (M-SHORAD) Battalions: There are already several of these battalions in service in Europe and elsewhere; the US Army wants to create four more. These units are employed against UAS, helicopters and aircraft. »

ABOVE: Rangers 'fast-rope' from a UH60 Blackhawk during the Best Ranger Competition at Fort Moore, Georgia. (US ARMY)

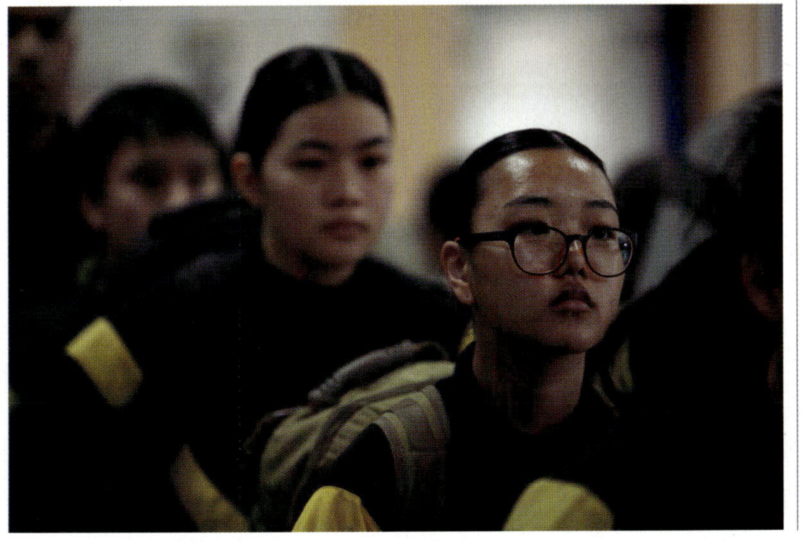

LEFT: Recruits for the New Jersey National Guard prepare for Basic Combat Training. After graduating they will join a local unit and serve for at least six years. (US ARMY)

Renamed US Army Installations

In Late 2023 the US Army renamed nine bases which previously were named for Confederate Generals of the US Civil War (1861-1865). We include this list to help readers become acquainted with the new names, which affected several well-known installations.

Old Name	New Name	Named for
Fort A.P. Hill, Virginia	Fort Walker	Dr Mary Walker, only female Medal of Honor recipient
Fort Benning, Georgia	Fort Moore	Korea and Vietnam War veteran Lt Gen Hal Moore and his wife, Julia, an advocate for military families
Fort Bragg, North Carolina	Fort Liberty	The value and concept of liberty
Fort Hood, Texas	Fort Cavazos	Gen Richard Cavazos, the US Army's first Hispanic four-star general, Korea and Vietnam veteran
Fort Lee, Virginia	Fort Gregg-Adams	Lt Gen Arthur Gregg, logistician and Lt Col Charity Adams, commander of the 6888th Central Postal Directory Battalion
Fort Pickett, Virginia	Fort Barfoot	Sgt (later Colonel) Van Barfoot, Medal of Honor recipient
Fort Polk, Louisiana	Fort Johnson	Sgt William H Johnson, Medal of Honor recipient
Fort Rucker, Alabama	Fort Novosel	Chief Warrant Officer Michael Novosel, Medal of Honor recipient
Fort Gordon, Georgia	Fort Eisenhower	General of the Army and 34th President of the United States Dwight D Eisenhower

It is notable the army is placing such increased effort on new air defence units. During the wars in Iraq and Afghanistan air defence capabilities atrophied due to the lack of an aerial threat and the other pressing needs of those conflicts. The army recognises that war against a peer opponent will mean a lack of air superiority, at least in the first weeks or months. The threat from UAS, suicide drones and loitering munitions has been proven in Ukraine and the Middle East. These new units bring air defence back to prominence as a major enabler of offensive power.

Brigade Combat Teams (BCTs) and smaller units are also experimenting with novel ways to use UAS, sensors, vehicles and other new items to sense, strike and survive. As the new capabilities are adopted, the army must determine where best to place them. For example, do new targeting capabilities best fit at company, battalion, or brigade levels, or all three in different ways? Should they be given to a scout platoon or incorporated into a weapons platoon or headquarters? The army does not know the final answers to such questions but is striving to find out by placing systems in the hands of soldiers at different levels.

Raising these new units requires the army to restructure, as it will need about 7,500 new billets. To create room for these billets and meet other transformation goals, the army is seeking to cut about 32,000 billets in total. According to the US Army's 2024 transformation white paper: "These planned reductions are to authorisations (spaces), and not to individual soldiers (faces). The army is not asking current soldiers to leave." Some soldiers will retrain for new occupational specialities while others will fill vacant billets.

Some of these changes are already underway. Some BCTs are losing their cavalry reconnaissance squadrons, while Infantry BCTs are seeing some weapons companies reduced to platoons. Billets are also being trimmed from other units, such as Security Force Assistance Brigades. Even Special Operations Forces (SOF) are being reduced by 3,000 billets. This move is controversial, as units don't want to lose the high-quality personnel typical in SOF. The army has countered by stating it needs less SOF forces for wars with peer opponents and it is focusing on eliminating billets which are historically often vacant or hard to fill anyway.

The army already struggles to meet recruiting goals, so there is no effort or desire to discharge serving soldiers. Instead, recruiting is getting bolstered to meet the increased demand for educated troops able to fill positions

RIGHT: Soldiers of the 41st Field Artillery Brigade fight with pugil sticks during a team-building exercise at Grafenwoehr, Germany. (US ARMY)

requiring technical skills. Recruiting Command can be a stressful posting for a soldier due to the demand to meet quotas and find quality candidates. Like other branches of the US military, the army has often fallen short of recruiting goals for several years.

As a result, Recruiting Command is being elevated to a 'three-star command,' led by a lieutenant general, who will report directly to the Secretary of the Army and Chief of Staff of the Army. There is a new warrant officer's position in recruiting along with a focus on new recruiting techniques which are more competitive in the current labour market. There are some successes, such as the Soldier Referral Program and Future Soldier Prep Course, both instituted in 2022. These programmes have brought over 14,000 recruits into the army since their inception.

Some units are being strengthened to face specific threats. One example is the 41st Field Artillery Brigade, stationed in Europe, reactivated in 2018 due to the increased Russian threat to NATO. As fielded, the brigade has two M270 MLRS battalions, each with two batteries with eight launchers each. This configuration was optimised for counterinsurgency operations. For better performance in peer-level conflict, the unit is being reconfigured with three batteries per battalion, each with nine launchers, a 40% increase in firepower. At least two other brigades are seeing the same upgrades.

These units are capable of long-range fires with missiles and rockets. The next goal is to equip them to engage an enemy force most effectively. Colonel Guy Yelverton, working within an acquisition group, said: "It's not about engaging as far out as possible with the most expensive round type to breathe a little easier. It might be letting that particular threat… come in a little closer so I can take it out with the right system … I can better utilise my entire suite of munitions and take on the full effect of the fight."

All this is happening because the US Army's leaders perceive growing threats. To them, the world seems more chaotic in the post-COVID world, particularly since the Ukraine War began. Gen George put it plainly, saying: "We understand how the battlefield has changed and how dangerous the world is. All you have to do is look at the news and see violence on every side of the globe." While the overall goal is deterrence, the army is preparing to win a war if it comes.

ABOVE: An M1A2 Abrams fires a 120mm cannon round during training. In combat a tank crew will quickly move to avoid return fire as enemy gunners will aim for the muzzle flash. (US ARMY)

US Army Strength 2024		
Component	Brigade Combat Teams	Personnel
Regular Army	31	443,000
National Guard	27	325,000
Army Reserve	0	190,000

LEFT: An M109A6 Paladin of the 1st Armored Division sends a 155mm high explosive round downrange during a deployment to South Korea. (US ARMY)

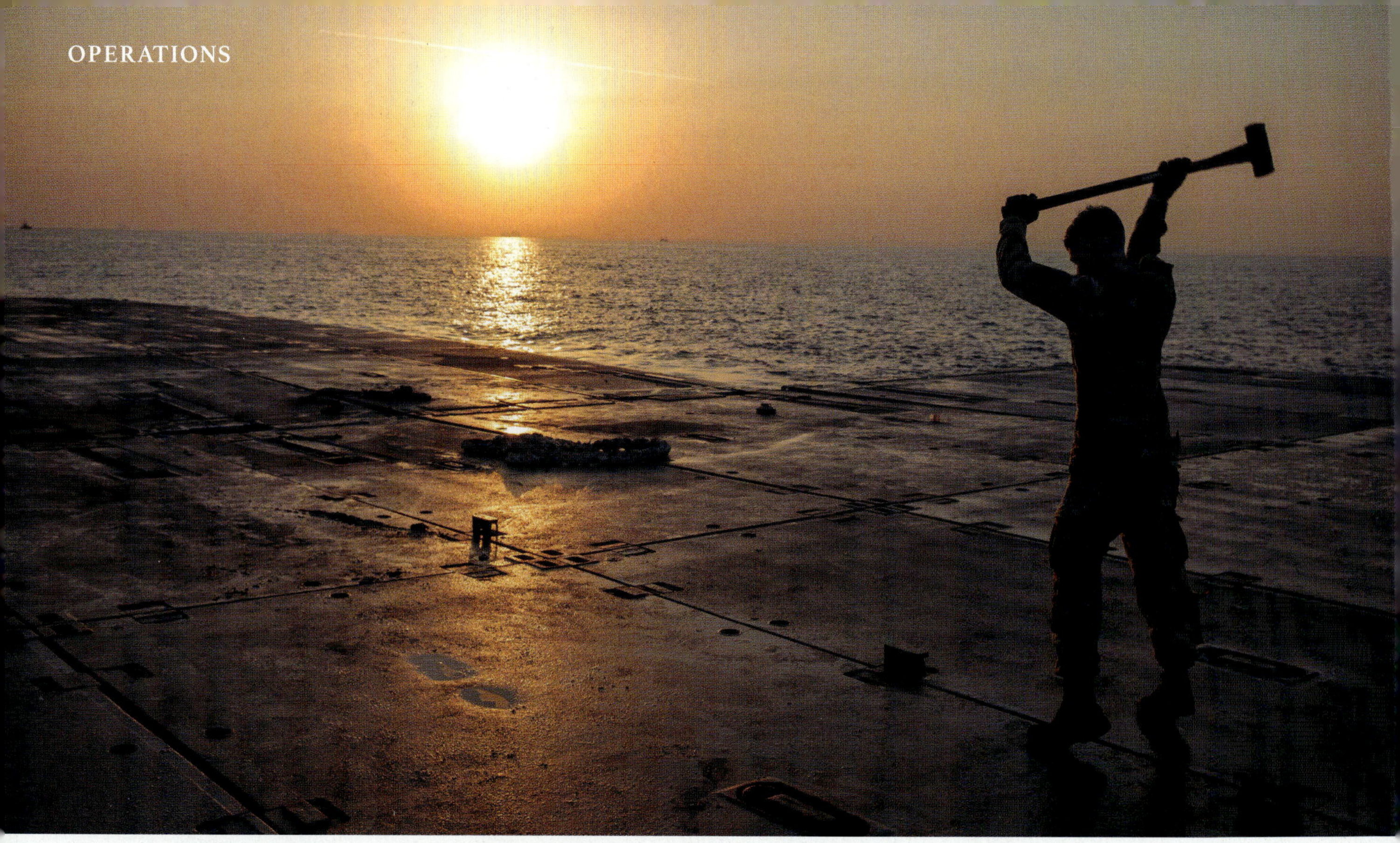

The Middle East

Conflict across the region

ABOVE: A soldier repairs the Trident Pier on the Gaza coast. This pier allowed relief supplies to reach Palestinians in need. (US ARMY)

Conflicts are ongoing across the Middle East and US Army troops are heavily involved in Israel, Syria, Iraq and elsewhere. While this is not a declared war, American troops are in combat operations, involving a mix of regular army and National Guard units which rotate through the region.

Israel: The conflict between Israel and Hamas-led militant groups in Gaza and Hezbollah-led groups in Lebanon, is ongoing. Israel has also been attacked by terror groups using drones and through missile and drone attacks directly from Iran. Since the Hamas attacks of October 7, 2023, the US has given approximately $18bn in security aid to Israel.

The United States has also provided relief aid to the Palestinians, including a portable pier system built and maintained by US Army engineers. The pier operated during May and June 2024 but was removed after aid organisations stopped using it. In October 2024, the US also committed an Army Terminal High Altitude Area Defense (THAAD) missile battery to Israel to help protect that nation from Iranian drone and missile strikes. The THAAD is effective against ballistic missiles and normally has six launchers which can each fire eight missiles before reloading. A THAAD battery normally has about 100 soldiers to operate it, and they are among the most frequently deployed type of army unit.

Syria/Iraq/Jordan: The US troops currently stationed in Syria and Iraq are there to help prevent the reformation of the so-called Islamic State or a follow-on group. They also work to limit the influence of Russia and Iran; both have substantial presence in war-torn Syria. Iran was using Syria to move weapons

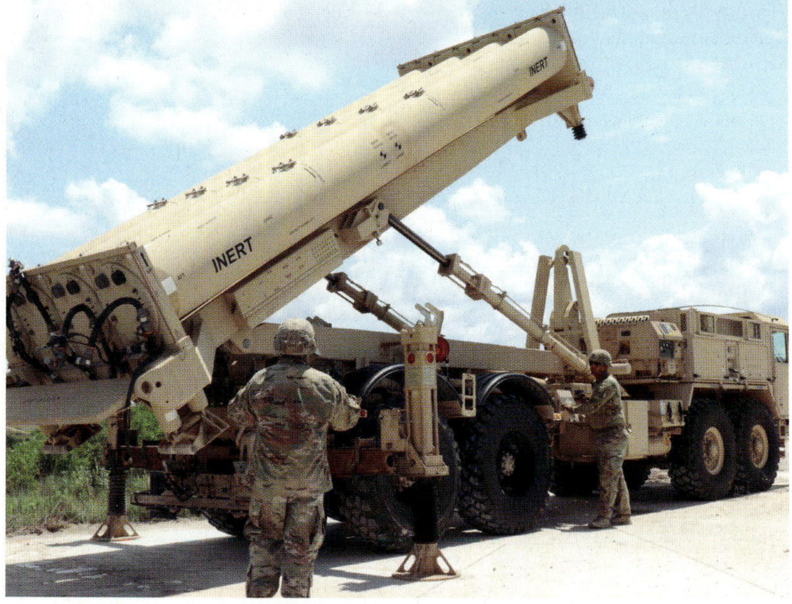

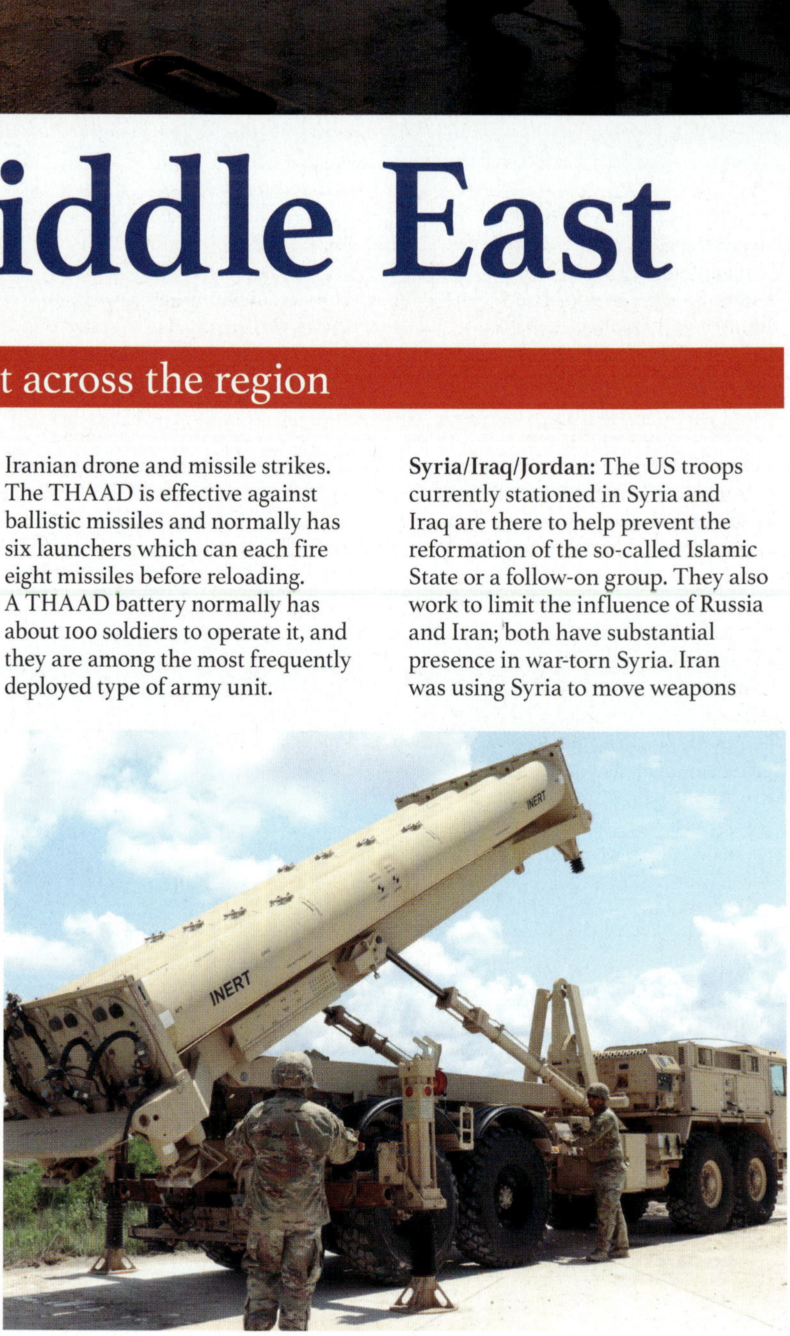

RIGHT: A THAAD air defence battery was moved to Israel in late 2024. This system has anti-ballistic missile capability. (US ARMY)

to Hezbollah in Lebanon, though US and allied efforts seem to have partially interdicted this route. The fall of the Assad regime in Syria in December 2024 means the situation there is evolving.

There are about 900 US troops in Syria and another 2,500 in Iraq, as of late 2024. US troops are currently scheduled to leave Iraq by the end of 2026. There are several thousand American troops in Jordan, including infantry and artillery units. These Army troops can call upon extensive air support when needed.

They come under frequent attacks by Iranian-backed proxy groups in the area, often with rockets and drones. A drone attack on a US outpost in Jordan called Tower 22 killed three soldiers from an Army Reserve unit. Twenty-seven other soldiers from four National Guard units were wounded in the attack. This was the first time US troops had been killed in an air attack in over 70 years. The drone is believed to have been an Iranian-built Shahed. Since October 2023 there have been over 200 attacks on US troops in the three nations.

A US base in northeastern Syria has been struck about 40 times alone. Mission Support Site Conoco is located near the Iraq border and a Syrian outpost with the same name, as well as a gas field. This is likely why it bears the name of an American oil company. The base is strategically located so Syrian and Iranian-backed groups attack it frequently.

The US retaliates often, using cannon and rocket artillery against opposing forces and their logistics and command and control nodes. US strikes in November 2024 caused heavy casualties among Iranian-backed groups.

Michael Knight is a senior fellow at the Washington Institute, a US-based Middle East thinktank. Speaking to the American military news service, Stars and Stripes, he stated the attacks against US troops and the American response have become cyclical: "For the third time this year [2024], we're probably in a cycle where [anti-American groups are] going to keep pushing the envelope," Knights said. "And then we're going to crack them a couple of times and then they're going to stop again for a while."

The US Army also operates several contingency and deterrence forces in the region, primarily operating out of Kuwait and Jordan. Task Force Spartan is the army component of Operation Spartan Shield and includes combat forces from the active and reserve components, with a heavy National Guard presence. The task force normally has about 10,000 troops in all, and they serve as a rapid-reaction force in the region, with heavy tank, infantry, artillery, and aviation assets.

ABOVE: A Chinook heavy transport helicopter carries paratroopers of the 82nd Airborne Division over Iraq and Syria en route to an undisclosed final location. (US ARMY)

LEFT: A 120mm mortar crew from the New Jersey National Guard's 44th Infantry BCT fires their weapon in Syria in July 2024. (US ARMY)

LEFT: A patrol from the 44th Infantry BCT covers Syrian Democratic Forces during a joint operation in Northeastern Syria in October 2024. (US ARMY)

Support to Ukraine

Weapons, equipment, and training

The US Army is heavily involved in training and supplying Ukrainian military forces during the current war. The forward-based training command in Europe under US 7th Army operates the Joint Multinational Training Group – Ukraine to provide needed training to Ukrainian troops, particularly on Western weapons and equipment. US Army Europe also operate the Security Assistance Group – Ukraine, a headquarters element responsible for coordinating support efforts with other NATO allies.

Much of the training mission has been fulfilled by National Guard units deploying to Grafenwoehr, Germany for tours of six months or more. In October 2024, the Pennsylvania National Guard's 56th Stryker BCT took over the mission from the Mississippi National Guard's 155th Armored BCT. These deployments generally consist of a few hundred troops from the committed unit, not the entire BCT.

In 2024 the US provided additional HIMARS, Bradley IFVs, Stryker infantry carrier, and other weapons and kit. Additionally, large amounts of ammunition, including the

ATACMS missile were transferred. The US is also purchasing ordnance which the Ukrainians already use, such as T-72 tanks, artillery ammunition for Soviet-calibre artillery, and even rockets for Ukraine's BM-21 Grad MLRS. In November 2024, the American government also eased restrictions on Ukrainian use of US-supplied weapons, allowing them to be used against targets inside Russia.

A Partial List of US Army and Foreign Weapons and Equipment Transferred to Ukraine	
Item	**Quantity**
Patriot air defence batteries and munitions	3
National Advanced Surface-to-Air Missile Systems	12
Stinger anti-aircraft missiles	3,000+
Counter-UAS systems	Numerous
HIMARS Rocket systems	40+
155mm howitzers	200+
155mm artillery rounds	3,077,000
105mm howitzers	72
105mm artillery rounds	800,000
Other artillery rounds (122/130/152/203mm)	490,000
81mm and 60mm mortars	300
Mortar rounds	700,000
122mm Grad rockets	60,000
Counter-artillery and counter-mortar radars	100+
Abrams tanks	31
T-72B Tanks	45
Bradley IFVs	300+
Stryker IFVs	400+
M113 armoured personnel carriers	900
M1117 armoured personnel carriers	400
MRAPs	1,000+
Javelin anti-armour systems	10,000
Other anti-armour weapons	120,000
TOW missiles	10,000
Small arms	50,000
Small arms ammunition and grenades (in rounds)	500,000,000

Source: US Dept of State as of December 14, 2024

North America

LEFT: A convoy of National Guardsmen makes its way down a flooded road in Florida. The author recalls driving a Humvee in a similar convoy after Hurricane Katrina in 2005. (US ARMY)

BELOW: A soldier launches a UAS during rescue operations along the French Broad River in North Carolina after Hurricane Helene. UAS help authorities determine where to focus their efforts after a disaster. (US ARMY)

Some of the US Army's biggest and most important real-world missions happen within the nation's borders. In 2024 a series of hurricanes struck the southeastern United States, causing hundreds of billions of dollars in damage and claiming hundreds of lives. Hurricanes Beryl, Debby, Francine, Helene, and Milton made landfall in the US between June and October. Helene and Milton caused the most fatalities and damage, requiring large governmental response.

Normally, disaster response is handled by the National Guard, as they are distributed throughout the states and can respond more quickly. They are also generally better equipped and trained for this mission. However, the amount of disruption, in particular that caused by Helene, meant some regular army troops were called on to assist as well.

Over 11,000 National Guardsmen were called to active service for the response. Over 18 states sent personnel, including some not affected by the storm. Often, these soldiers are volunteers with specialities needed by the relief forces.

The hurricanes caused widespread heavy rains, flooding, power outages and in a few cases, tornadoes sprouting from the storm's outer wind bands. Guard units deployed as soon as the weather clears enough to make relief efforts practical. They conduct search and rescue operations, clear roads of debris, set up distribution points for food and clean water, giving medical aid and assisting local police in maintaining order and arresting looters.

As examples, the Florida Guard's 1-230th Assault Helicopter Battalion rescued over 100 people trapped by floodwaters and delivered water, food, and electrical generators. The unit also surveyed roads, dams, and bridges to help prioritise repair work. Meanwhile, the Virginia National Guard sent two companies of troops with tactical trucks and helicopter support. These troops helped local authorities to clear roads and rescue citizens.

The 101st Airborne Division of the regular army also sent a detachment to assist in relief efforts after Helene. While these troops were not as well equipped for this mission type as the Guardsmen they worked with, they did make use of some of the new systems the division has been testing (see page 34). This included UAS and the new Infantry Squad Vehicle (IVS).

ABOVE: A cavalry scout from the 1st Armored Division launches a Black Hornet Soldier-Borne Sensor during an exercise in Poland. This hand-held UAS provides an infantry squad its own reconnaissance ability. (US ARMY)

Continuous Transformation

Balancing action and preparation

The US Army does not want to be too late to the next war. It cannot afford to be. General Douglas MacArthur, a controversial but competent officer, wrote that most failures in war were due to an army being too late in comprehending a new threat, too late in recognising the danger, and too late in its preparations to combat that new threat. The plan to prevent such a failure is called Continuous Transformation.

The first step in the US Army's preparation for future warfare is called 'Transformation in Contact', and it puts new and emerging technologies into soldiers' hands now, so they can begin learning to use it right away. The term comes from the Army Chief of Staff, General Randy George. At a speech delivered to the Association of the United States Army (AUSA) on October 15, 2024, Gen George announced this effort has been advanced to the

RIGHT: General James Rainey took over Army Futures Command on October 4, 2022. (US ARMY)

'Transformation in Contact 2.0' stage, which expands the effort to more army units, including two divisions, two armoured brigade combat teams, two Stryker brigade combat teams, and other units in the National Guard and Army Reserve (see page 18).

George believes these efforts are vital as adversaries seek to drive wedges between the US and its allies and increase distrust and chaos. "Today the world is even more dangerous and ambiguous. Our army remains incredibly busy,"

George stated. "...at the same time, we see our adversaries are adapting by working together. Russia, China, Iran and North Korea represent an axis of upheaval."

Beyond expanding the Transformation in Contact initiative, the US Army plans to focus on three areas in 2025. First, the army wants to improve troops ability to engage the enemy's uncrewed systems. It also seeks to improve the accuracy and range of its long-range precision weapon systems. While strides have been made in cannon, rocket and missile systems, further upgrades are needed.

Lastly, the army's industrial base must be strengthened and modernised, an ongoing effort from the previous years. Many predicted the Ukraine War would be over in weeks or a few months at most; instead, it is in its third year with no end in sight. The US Army needs an industrial base which can expand production of munitions and other expendable equipment. It must also have the depth to develop new systems while keeping the current ones operational.

As of writing, General James E. Rainey leads US Army Futures Command, charged with overseeing these efforts to create the future army. There are three major obstacles to his command's efforts. The first is the speed of change. He said: "The amount of technical disruption in the character of war is unprecedented, and it just continues to go faster and faster. Whatever you think you know this year, come back in 90 days, and

you'll know something different." Rainey also wrote: "Because armies adapt, new technology is rarely decisive in the ways people predict. But it is disruptive in that it changes how military forces operate, organize, and equip."

The second challenge is the need to balance current operations and needs against future requirements, many of which are not fully understood. Rainey defines a capability simply as: "the ability to do something on the battlefield." Technology by itself does not provide capability. That technology must be integrated with personnel, doctrine, training and leadership, among other things.

This takes time and effort for units which are already busy on current training exercises, deployments and support to allies.

Third, the US Army's acquisition process needs improvement so new technologies and weapons can be created and adopted quickly. Currently, it can take years or even more than a decade for major new systems to be funded, designed, tested and fielded. Technology advances quickly in the 21st century, so that programmes are often disrupted and increased in cost by new requirements that must be added in the middle of the effort. The current processes are long, bureaucratic »

ABOVE: A platoon sergeant from a Robotics and Autonomous Systems Platoon caries a Ghost-X UAS into position prior to launch. (US ARMY)

LEFT: Purple smoke surrounds an infantry fire team as it advances with a Ghost-60 robotic dog. The robot acts as a scout for its human handlers. (US ARMY)

and complex and cannot match the fast pace of modern warfare. While those processes are overall sound and logical, they lack the flexibility for fast movement and adaptation. This is a problem not just for the army but the US military as a whole.

Continuous Transformation is divided into three phases. The aforementioned Transformation in Contact mainly focuses on capabilities the army needs in the next two years or less. This includes new UAS and battle command systems which allow soldiers to blend different systems together for battlefield use. New systems thought to have potential value are placed into the hands of soldiers now, who are encouraged to find how they are useful and develop their tactical use during training and exercises.

"In many cases, we are allowing the aspirational to stand in the way of the doable. There are technologies that would be useful in our formations right now but are not yet fielded because we are waiting until they can do even more," Rainey describes. "New technologies with game-changing potential should be in operational units as soon as they are useful, even if only in small quantities of minimum-viable products. This accelerates development of the technology, but it also lets us learn how to best employ it and how to adapt our formations and training accordingly. Most importantly, it gives leaders experience using the technology as it evolves."

Gen Rainey describes the next phase, called 'Deliberate Transformation', as: "efforts managed through army-level processes to deliver the army we need within the time horizon for defence programming." This level aims for a two-to-seven-year timeframe, which coincides with the US Department of Defense budget planning cycle.

Overarching Transformation in Contact and Deliberate Transformation is 'Concept-Driven Transformation', which is the US Army's longer-term vision for preparing and equipping its forces. This phase includes consideration of near-term goals but also looks out to perhaps 15 years. However, the timelines mentioned for each phase are not rigid. The concept considers that technological changes will be happening concurrently with the army's plans, forcing it to adapt to new systems and concepts while modifying or even abandoning those which have been overcome by new developments.

When a cutting-edge technology seems at least minimally useful, it should be fielded, if only to a few units, allowing soldiers to get their hands on it. Once they determine the practicality and potential of the technology, then it can be acquired in greater quantity and worked into the army's training and organisation. New technologies, such as command and control devices and software, are like the technology used by civilians today. It is designed for periodic upgrades and improvements. This allows for repeated improvements after adoption.

Bringing the whole concept together requires focus on more than just technology. Gen Rainey writes that capabilities don't simply come from technology, but the formations that use them. This means soldiers, who are in the end the ones who will make the concept work: weapons, robots, software and all. Success requires changes and cooperation across Doctrine, Organisation, Training, Materiel, Leadership and Education, Personnel, Facilities, and Policy (DOTMLPF-P). This rather ungainly acronym will see little use outside army planning circles but does concisely describe the breadth and depth to which army leaders must be prepared to depart from old and outmoded thinking from the past two decades.

BELOW: A Family of Counter Unmanned Systems (FoCUS) operates during a Project Convergence exercise at Fort Irwin, California. FoCUS is a medium range, day or night counter UAS system. (US ARMY)

To make this work in a war with a near-peer adversary, the US Army is already strengthening the division as the basic fighting unit, abandoning the prior Brigade Combat Teams (BCT)-centric doctrine which worked well during the war on terror but fails in a large-scale war. Each division controls two to four BCTs currently. These BCTs operated almost as small divisions, with extensive support elements for the combat troops.

Over time this made them cumbersome; an Infantry BCT has about 4,300 troops under the old system of organisation. A new design reduces the same BCT to about 3,000 soldiers. To retain combat power these BCTs will make more use of UAS and other unmanned systems. Major General Brett Sylvia, commander of the 101st Airborne Division, states that: "As we transition to a mobile brigade combat team, we take out many of those manned platforms and make them unmanned platforms with new constructs. We're able to trade steel for blood."

Different units are testing new concepts for future dispersion to the entire Army. The 101st Airborne Division took UAS and electronic warfare lessons from the Ukraine War and put them through a major exercise at Fort Johnson, Louisiana (see page 34). The 3rd Infantry Division at Fort Stewart, Georgia, is developing new UAS tactics. The 20th Engineer Brigade at Fort Liberty, North Carolina, is using robotic systems to create new methods for breaching obstacles on the battlefield.

The US Army's transformation concept seems complicated because it is. The plan requires leaders who are flexible in mind and trusting of subordinates to make it all work. Leaders at all levels will have to mentor their subordinates to understand the overall intent and orders while acting to carry them out on their own initiative. Units which must disperse and limits their communications traffic will not often be able to call their higher headquarters for instructions. This method of delegation, known as Mission Command, will be vital for success on the envisioned battlefields of the coming decades.

Mobile Brigade Combat Teams

ABOVE: A sergeant directs a Squad Automatic Weapon gunner toward his assigned zone of fire in their newly established perimeter during training at Fort Johnson, Louisiana. (US ARMY)

The US Army's transformation programme recognises that Brigade Combat Teams (BCTs) will need to operate in a dispersed fashion to avoid enemy fire in a war with a near-peer adversary. They must also be able to hide in different types of terrain. This is more difficult if the unit is large, with hundreds of vehicles and many tons of heavy equipment.

Along with testing new systems that are smaller and lighter, the army is also experimenting with new unit organisation. The mobile BCT is a concept for a unit which has over 25% fewer troops (4,300 versus 3,000) and is more flexible than current BCTs. It is well-equipped with tools for fighting in the electromagnetic spectrum and against UAS. It also uses its own UAS to find and strike enemy formations.

New technology also allows smaller groups of soldiers to perform tasks which normally require more personnel. For example, experiments with command posts have reduced the number of soldiers needed to run them operationally from 60 to eight. Some tasks are being elevated to the division level, allowing BCTs to concentrate more on fighting.

So far, three units are reorganised as mobile BCTs, all of them light infantry formations. These include the 2nd Brigade, 101st Airborne Division at Fort Campbell, Kentucky, the 2nd Brigade, 25th Infantry Division in Hawaii and the 3rd Brigade, 10th Mountain Division at Fort Drum, New York. The mobile BCTs have new subordinate units, such as the Multi-Functional Reconnaissance Company (MFRC, see page 20).

The 101st's brigade is the farthest along in the process and conducted two exercises in 2024 to put its new ideas into practice. This brigade is using the new Infantry Squad Vehicle (ISV), an unarmoured but nimble transport which allows squads to carry more supplies than they could on foot. The ISV can be sling-loaded by the division's helicopters. It also has smaller command posts with only five wheeled vehicles and a small remote antenna farm, making it harder to find and target. It can set up and break down quickly, so it can move often.

The brigade's second exercise saw it move over 500 miles by helicopter airlift. According to the 101st Division's commander, Major General Brett Sylvia, being able to move that distance puts most critical locations in Iran, North Korea, China, or Russia within range from existing regional bases. As the mobile BCT concept is refined, more units will be converted to their table of organisation.

RIGHT: Air defence against UAS is a vital need for BCTs. This soldier loads the .50-calibre machine gun on an Avenger air defence vehicle. (US ARMY)

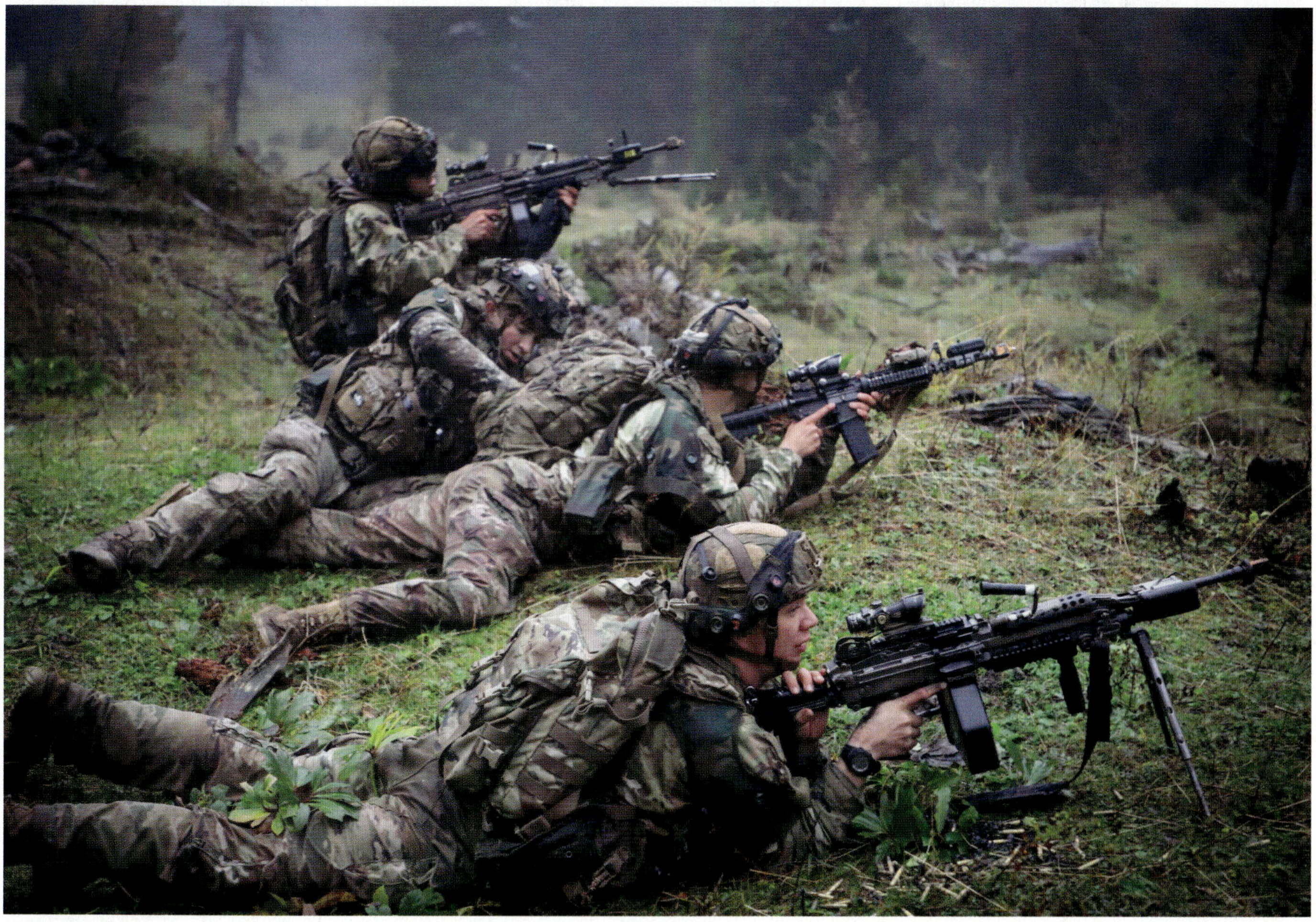

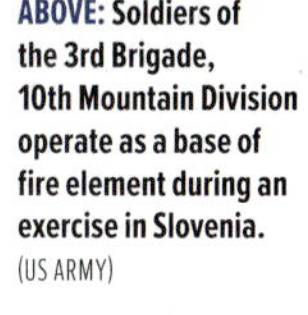

The 3rd Brigade, 10th Mountain Division is also using the ISV and experimenting with UAS and electronic warfare, but they are also testing new small unit organisations. In late 2024 the BCT's troops in Eastern Europe put their ideas to use. They decentralised the brigade's sustainment battalion, so it is harder to detect and target. The brigade also created three 'strike companies,' a mixed force of scouts, UAS (including armed drones), counter-UAS teams, electronic warfare teams and mortar squads. These companies are testing new combat techniques in preparation for a major exercise at the Joint Multinational Readiness Centre in Germany in early 2025.

In 2025, the US Army will begin spreading this concept to two armoured and two Stryker brigades. While these types of BCTs will not be as light due to their armoured vehicles and heavier equipment sets, they will receive new unmanned systems and command and control systems to enable better battlefield performance. It made sense for the army to use light infantry units for its initial experiments, as they are smaller and more lightly equipped; they also will benefit more from the new technologies in terms of relative combat power.

However, armoured and Stryker BCTs must also be modernised and brought into the new transformation scheme. A light infantry BCT is not always the best choice, depending on the environment. For example, light units are generally good choices for a jungle environment in the southern Pacific region, while the open plains of eastern Europe are good tank country. All BCTs must be brought up to the same standards and equipped similarly to be completely interoperable. The army learned this lesson recently when a BCT of the 82nd Airborne Division was issued with new networking equipment, it could no longer communicate with the other units which still used the older versions of the system.

Two divisions will also start transforming in 2025. They are a vital part of this process. To increase the mobility and focus of BCTs, many logistical and support functions are moving to the divisional level. This means the BCTs need their parent division to enable them to focus on combat operations. Conversely, the divisions need to learn how best to organise and support their subordinate BCTs.

ABOVE: Soldiers of the 3rd Brigade, 10th Mountain Division operate as a base of fire element during an exercise in Slovenia. (US ARMY)

LEFT: A 10th Mountain Division soldier operates a Skydio drone, demonstrating its ability to provide real-time video to troops in the field. (US ARMY)

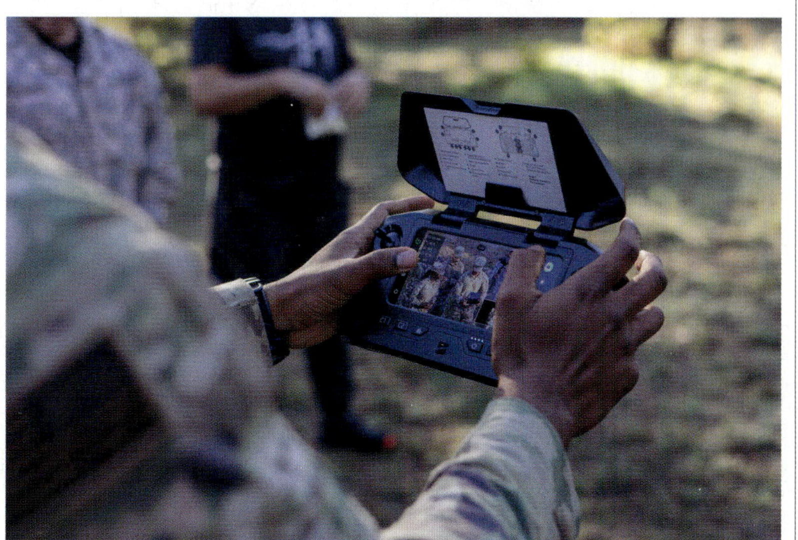

Multi-Functional Reconnaissance Company

New concept in scouting the enemy

At the ground level, the US Army's transformation efforts are delivering new types of units able to integrate and adopt new technologies, testing them for potential widespread adoption. One such formation is the Multi-Functional Reconnaissance Company (MFRC). It is equipped with the latest in commercial UAS, electronic warfare equipment, counter-UAS systems and command and control integration devices.

Many of the new technologies finding use in the Ukraine War are not weapons themselves. Artillery systems, for example, are not significantly more powerful in terms of explosive power than they were 50 years ago. What has made them more lethal are the reconnaissance, targeting, and guidance systems which allow artillery units to strike more quickly and with great accuracy. UAS and electronic warfare detection systems are two major tools which enable greater lethality.

The MFRC's job is to test all of its new equipment, figure out if it works, and then evaluate the best way to use it. The company contains five platoons. One is the Robotics and Autonomous Systems (RAS) platoon, which operates UAS and ground-based drones and robots. Next is a drone and electronic warfare platoon and there are three reconnaissance platoons referred to as 'hunter-killer platoons.'

These platoons are liberally issued equipment to experiment with new techniques. Each hunter-killer platoon has up to six commercial UAS to use for hunting targets. Sergeants and officers in the platoon each have a chest mounted Android phone loaded with the Tactical Assault Kit (TAK). Software in the phone includes mapping technology to mark enemy positions and communicate by voice or text message. A software called Sentinel AI helps create a suitable call for fire to friendly artillery. This reduces the time needed for a fire mission from a previous eight minutes to less than a minute. The TAK also has satellite communications capability.

Each platoon also has a guidance unit for Switchblade 600 loitering munitions. This munition is portable but bulky, so they are kept at the brigade headquarters. When a target is found, the brigade can launch the Switchblade in the proper direction. The platoon then takes control of the munition and guides it to the target.

LEFT: Finding the enemy still requires scouts using their eyes and ears, like these two scout observers of the MFRC. (US ARMY)

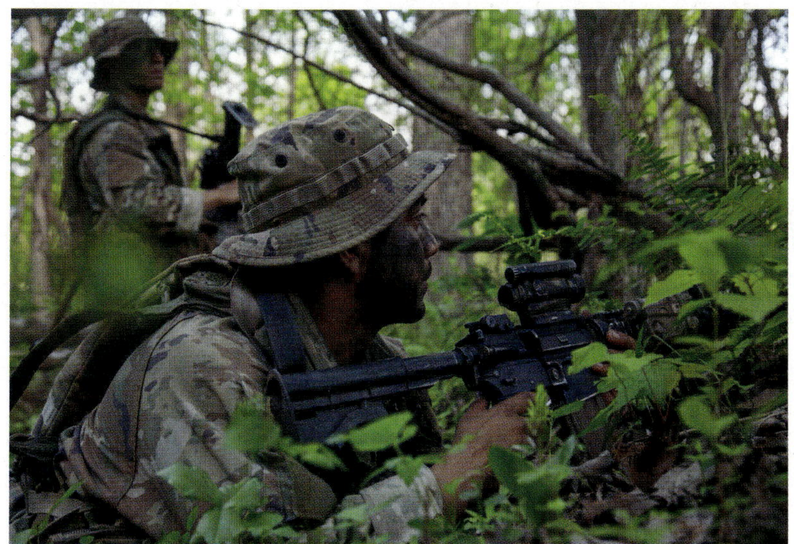

To combat enemy UAS, each platoon has a Bal Chatri UAS detector and a Dronebuster anti-UAS rifle. Soldiers also have a backpack-carried device which can detect enemy radar systems. The RAS Platoon uses the PDW C100 UAS, which has reconnaissance capabilities but can also carry ordnance to drop on enemy positions. These small munitions resemble 60mm mortar rounds and are similar to systems seen in use in Ukraine. This platoon also uses the General Dynamics Small Multipurpose Equipment Transport (SMET), a wheeled ground robot used to carry cargo and recharge the platoon's various electrically powered systems. They are also testing the Silent Tactical Energy Enhanced Dismount (STEED), an electrically assisted wheelbarrow-like system which can handle 500lb loads for up to 30 miles.

The MFRC is equipped with the new M1301 Infantry Squad Vehicle (ISV), a light transport based on the Chevrolet Colorado ZR2 off road pickup. The ISV carries up to nine soldiers and can be transported by both the Blackhawk and Chinook helicopters. The amount of supplies an ISV can carry doubles the time each recce element can stay in the field to six days.

The MFRC in the 101st Airborne Division's 2nd Brigade was formed in March 2024 and went with the brigade for a major exercise in August (see page 34). This was the unit's first major exercise, which took place at the Joint Readiness Training Center at Fort Johnson, Louisiana.

The exercise provided an opportunity to test the MFRC's proposed tactics and techniques. Not everything went to plan, which was itself instructive and valuable. For example, soldiers learned that the TAK signal can be detected and targeted, so they learned to limit their use. There were also problems with transmitting video footage from UAS, which the troops could not get to work. It is notable the Ukrainians solved this problem by using Chinese drones, which the US Army cannot adopt.

There were also problems with the Bal Chatri drone detector which failed to locate UAS. One of the platoon leaders realised the detector was ignoring all American-made drones, considering them as friendly. This was an important lesson.

Other methods succeeded. On the first day, a platoon used its UAS to find three enemy cannon artillery systems. A quickly coordinated mock strike by friendly HIMARS artillery destroyed them. They went on to destroy 29 different pieces of equipment in the first day using UAS to guide artillery.

Another success came from small bags the MFRC made, each containing a small number of Raspberry Pi single board computers. Soldiers hung them in trees, where they put out electronic emissions similar to a command post. When the opposing force targeted them, it revealed the positions of their artillery for counterbattery fire.

BELOW: Soldiers gather around their ISV transport. Though not in view, they are using a Signal Harvest system, which detects Wi-Fi and Bluetooth signals. (US ARMY)

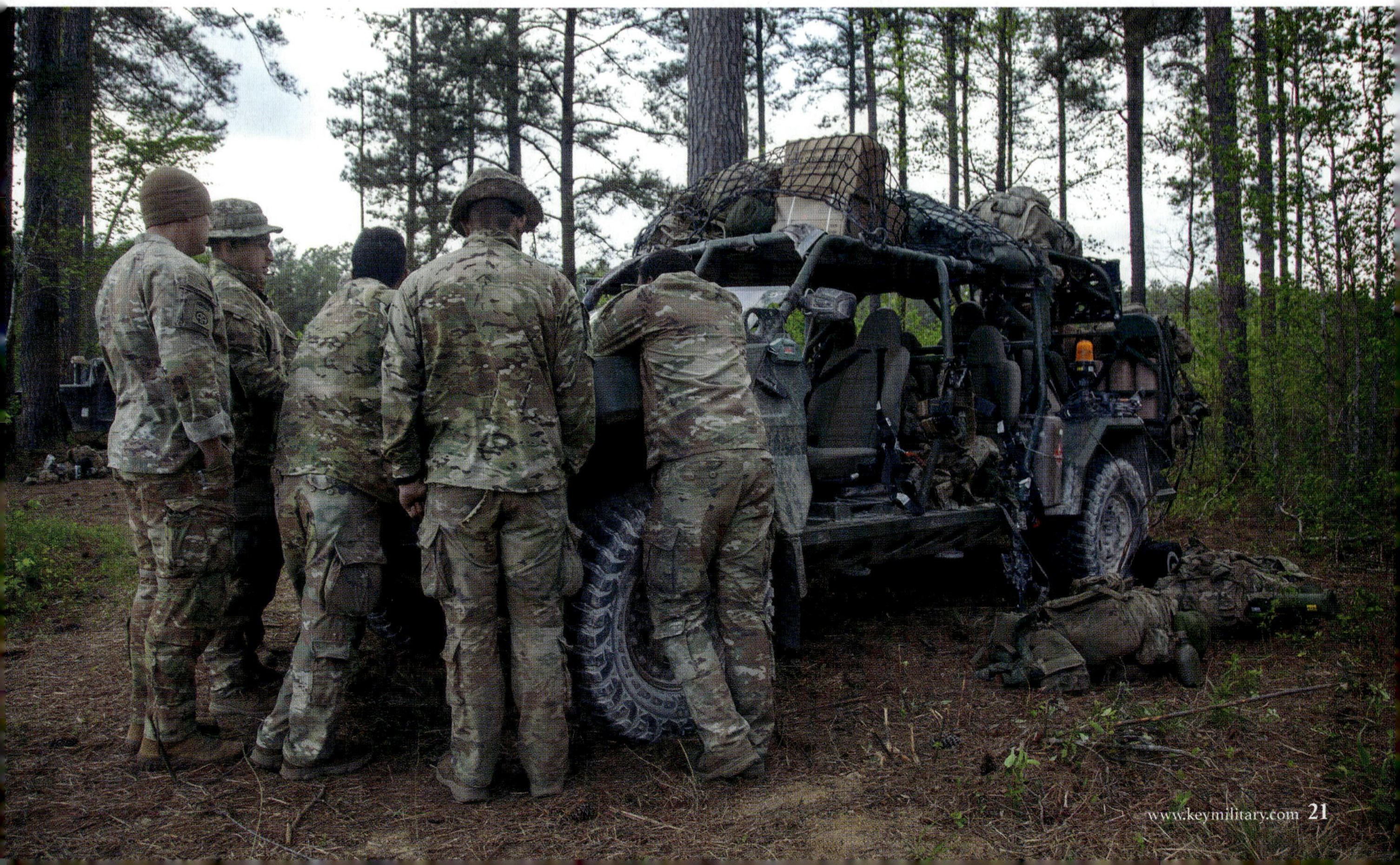

Human-Machine Integration

RIGHT: An autonomous UH60 Blackhawk picks up a sling load during a test mission. These aircraft can be operated from hundreds of miles away. Note this UH60 has a pilot aboard in case of malfunction during testing. (US ARMY)

BELOW: An unmanned, eight-wheeled, all-electric, robotic vehicle armed with the R600 autonomous weapon system provides support to dismounted soldiers at Fort Irwin, California. (US ARMY)

UAS are well integrated into combat operations, but they generally have an operator and armed systems have a human controller who determines whether it can fire. This is known as 'human in the loop' control. However, the technology for weapons to operate fully autonomously, even making targeting decisions, is in full development across the globe. The US Army is working on its own versions of this deadly new tech.

For the foreseeable future, any armed system will continue to be administered by a human operator and will lack the ability to fire unless directed by a soldier. This is a US Department of Defense policy intended to prevent tragedies involving this new but untested technology. Whether this policy will ever change is a matter for speculation. In the meantime, the US Army is experimenting with armed and unarmed platforms and how soldiers might best use them. The term the army uses is Human Machine Integrated Formations (HMIF).

There are advantages to autonomous systems. Battlefields are dangerous places and machines can assume some of the riskier missions instead of humans. These include reconnaissance, armed overwatch, frontline resupply, casualty evacuation and Explosive Ordnance Disposal (EOD). There is a strong imperative to improve combat unit's use of and effectiveness through HMIF. In the words of retired USAF Colonel Dawn Zoldi: "Why? Because robots don't bleed."

Gone are the days of mass conscript armies as in the 20th century. Modern

armies are smaller and thus cannot withstand heavy personnel losses as well. Advanced militaries require time to train troops properly, especially with high-tech weapons. For example, Russia has so far been able to recruit significant numbers of new soldiers, but their casualty rates often exceed 1,000 per day, partly because their military lacks time for proper training before committing many recruits to battle. Using robotic systems to assume some of that risk is one way to preserve human capital.

Some of the US Army's initial thinking considered robots replacing humans on the battlefield, but that idea raised concerns about the dangers of autonomous systems acting without oversight. The concept soon changed to using robotic platforms alongside soldiers. The US Army is using an experimentation force called EXFOR to develop the new techniques and tactics of HMIF in combat. EXFOR is run by the Maneuver Battle Lab (MBL), an army agency focused on new technologies for combat arms units. The army established EXFOR around 2004 to study modernisation and has recently focused it solely on HMIF development. This formation includes seasoned veterans as well as

soldiers just out of basic training, just as in a line unit. This allows it to test how quickly even novice soldiers can learn to work within the HMIF.

Other units from across the army are also committing detachments to work with EXFOR at places such as the National Training Center at Fort Irwin in the California desert. This enables the force as a whole to learn

about these new robotic systems and for them to contribute their own ideas and observations. Special Forces, Rangers, infantry, and armour units are among the unit types which are training with robotic systems.

Retired Colonel Christopher Willis heads the MBL and has a plan for how to get HMIF into the field. He said: "I'm going to give a platoon to a battalion, and then that platoon can focus on tactics, techniques, and procedures. In the future, at some point, the army will then start creating these platoons out in the force." He sees such platoons as part of a battalion headquarters company or a weapons company, where its assets could be pushed down to the company level, not unlike the way in which a mortar platoon's fire support or medics operate now.

Early experiments are indicating that soldiers will need a change in mindset. According to EXFOR's commander, Captain Tim Young, some soldiers: "try to put their forces out and then try to preserve the robots, but that's not the intent of the robots. You have to shift your mindset, push the robots out, because there's no reason we should shed human blood on first contact." Since robotic systems are major items of equipment, soldiers seemed naturally reluctant to risk their issued equipment for fear of not being able to get it replaced. In the end, however, robots are expendable.

Many of these systems were tested at the army's latest Project Convergence event in 2024. This exercise tests how to best integrate and use new technologies. These included an autonomous UH-60 Blackhawk helicopter, US and British Army versions of an armed robotic combat vehicle, Ghost robotic dogs and an unarmed robotic transport used for resupply and casualty evacuation.

LEFT: Infantrymen receive cover from an armed robotic vehicle while working with a Ghost robotic dog, which provides reconnaissance capability and can act like a sentry, warning its unit of threats. (US ARMY)

LEFT: A robotic combat vehicle armed with an M240 7.62mm machine gun provides overwatch to infantry in an urban combat exercise. (US ARMY)

BELOW: The British Army regularly participates in Project Convergence and in 2024 brought their own autonomous combat vehicle. (US ARMY)

Preparing for War in Europe

The price of deterrence

RIGHT: A Stryker Dragoon of the 2nd Armored Cavalry Regiment a unit stationed in Germany, takes part in an exercise in North Macedonia. (US ARMY)

Though Russia is currently fully engaged in its war in Ukraine, NATO remains concerned about the threat Russia poses to Europe in both the short and long terms. Not all of Russia's combat power is committed to Ukraine and the Russian military has shown considerable capability both of rebuilding forces degraded in combat and in raising new units. Russia has always shown a degree of 'latent power' in its ability to persevere in wartime despite massive losses, however grim the situation may look for them on paper. NATO does not want its eastern flank to become the next war zone.

The end goal is deterrence, so that no war occurs, but there are challenges to achieving that desired state. The 'peace dividend' after the Cold War ended led some nations to reduce defence spending, which lowered the modernity and readiness of their militaries. NATO has incorporated many new nations over the past few decades, many of whom were former Soviet-bloc states. These nations are upgrading their armies to come up to NATO

standards, but this takes time. It also takes time to brings these disparate forces together into a coherent whole.

The US Army is acting to achieve that state of coherence within NATO and be ready if a conflict arises. Toward that end, it is working with NATO partners at all levels. The army knows that victory in a European war will come only through coordinated operations with allies. General Daryl

Williams, commander of US Army Europe and Africa, put it simply: "The US cannot do it alone."

Partnership efforts have expanded significantly since the Ukraine War began. The US Army has long worked closely with nations like the UK and France, both of which conduct operations worldwide and can project power. It has also worked closely with longtime NATO members such as Germany and Italy and been involved

BELOW: Getting weapons and equipment to where they are needed is a major undertaking in crowded Europe. This heavy equipment transporter is carrying an Abrams tank of the 3rd Infantry Division in Lithuania. (US ARMY)

in the effort to integrate and upgrade the armies of newer members in eastern and southeastern Europe. After Russia invaded Ukraine, the need to establish a credible deterrent force became paramount. The US Army has done this through two primary means.

The first is training. Soldier skills have to be built and maintained through hard, realistic training. By carrying out joint training events with NATO partners, US Army troops understand how the NATO troops on their flanks will operate. This has an added benefit to the US Army in keeping it from becoming too wedded to its own doctrine and tactics. US Army troops frequently report learning much from training events, picking up new techniques from their training partners. These events include urban warfare training, tank and artillery gunnery ranges, and the occasional competition, such as the International Tank Challenge.

Exercises are the second way in which the US Army prepares for war. Armies which train together are able to operate together. This is especially important for NATO, as many of its member states do not have armies large enough to commit substantial stand-alone forces, such as brigades and divisions. However, these nations would commit smaller forces as part of NATO joint task forces. Large joint exercises allow NATO to discover how best to employ its varied ground forces and where US Army units would be used most effectively.

Major annual exercises in Europe include Saber Junction, held in the Joint Multinational Readiness Centre in Hohenfels, Germany, and Arctic Challenge, which has included army troops as the Arctic becomes a more likely battleground. A number of exercises are included under the

Defender series, including Steadfast Defender, in 2024 the largest NATO exercise since the Return of Forces to Germany (REFORGER) exercises of the Cold War. The US Army also takes part in NATO exercises which occur outside Europe but within NATO spheres of interest. In 2025 these include Flintlock 25 and African Lion in Africa.

US Army preparation includes exercises within the Continental United States (CONUS). In mid-2024 the 1st Armored Division completed a large-scale exercise at Fort Irwin, California, home of the National Training Center (NTC). The army realised it needed to exercise divisions as much as the brigades. According to III Corps operations officer Colonel Ted Stokes: "Really, a brigade is looking at mastering the close fight, tank on tank, Bradley on infantry fighting vehicle. A division approaches the fight much differently. They've got a lot of sensors collection, a lot of fires capability to shape the enemy force before they get into the close fight."

There are still many challenges to a potential war in Europe and NATO joint operations are a work in progress. As General Williams states: "I cannot take a Norwegian grenade and put it into a Swedish tube before qualifying and sorting out the ballistics. The nitty-gritty details matter." Nevertheless, US Army leadership is confident of the outcome of any aggression from Russia's president, Vladimir Putin. According to Williams: "He's going to get a fist sandwich in his mouth. He will find a very viable force ready to defend and defeat him there. He'll find someone that's ready to go."

ABOVE: The European landscape is divided by large rivers. These soldiers of the 36th Engineer Brigade are using an M30 Bridge Erection Boat to construct a ribbon bridge in Poland. (US ARMY)

BELOW: Troops from the Forward Land Forces Battle Group Poland pose for a photograph during a joint exercise. This battle group includes troops from the United States, United Kingdom, Croatia, and Romania. (US ARMY)

Preparing for War in the Pacific

Power projection, vast distances, and a network of allies

ABOVE: A high-altitude balloon system floats into the air after launching in the Philippines. Such balloon systems provide added communication and surveillance capability to operational forces. (US ARMY)

It is a widely accepted idea that a war in the Pacific will primarily involve naval and air power, with ground forces limited to Marines and perhaps a few army assets in support. While there is truth to the role of naval and air forces across the vast distances of the Pacific Ocean, history shows that army forces would play a larger role than many believe. Millions of army troops fought in the Pacific during World War Two and army forces were paramount in the Korean and Vietnam wars. The US Army understands this and is preparing for its role in any future war in the Pacific region.

Army preparations for conflict are part of the US military's overall joint concept for war in the region. They are designed to work with and alongside American naval and air forces as well as the militaries of allies. Critics state the army is trying to justify budget allocations, but its arguments bear analysis, and its efforts are seeing success in several areas.

In the event of a crisis, US Army forces will need to be quickly forward deployed to critical terrain. In the Pacific, this generally means

islands and the Korean Peninsula, itself a sort of island since North Korea holds the northern portion of it. The advantage of an island is it cannot be sunk. Army forces placed on one can move, hide, or harden

RIGHT: A soldier of the 25th Infantry Division uses his night-vision device in concert with a laser-aiming device on his M4 carbine during joint training in the Philippines. The laser can only be seen through the night-vision optic. (US ARMY)

their positions against enemy attack. Units such as the Multi-Domain Task Force (MDTF), which has land attack, anti-ship, air defence and electronic warfare capabilities, can deny a radius around the island to

Company Level UAS

Situational awareness for infantry squaddies

LEFT: A PDW C-100 is launched by a fire team. The drone's carrying case can be seen at lower right. (PDW)

Unmanned Aerial Systems (UAS) have proven their value across many conflicts but have previously been limited to use by the higher echelons of command to provide battlefield awareness which is then disseminated to subordinates as needed. However, this takes time and there can be differences in what a brigade staff thinks are useful versus what a company commander needs at that moment. The current wars in Ukraine and the Middle East have shown their utility at all levels of combat formations from division down to squad.

The US Army has been a decades-long user of UAS, but mostly at the brigade and above. As part of the service's transformation efforts, UAS are now being distributed down to company and even platoon and squad level. This is largely due to the proliferation of drone technology worldwide and the miniaturisation not only of the drones but of the technology for small, high-resolution cameras and sensors. Companies and smaller elements can only carry so much equipment and are already overloaded, so new UAS must be compact and lightweight enough to be practical.

As the US Army evaluated the technologies which will best fit its needs, it released a requirement for a small UAS to be issued to company-sized units, providing them with their own Surveillance and Reconnaissance, Surveillance and Target Acquisition (RSTA) assets. This requirement, called Tranche 1, allows troops to experiment with the new technology and figure out how best to use it.

In September 2024, the army announced the selection of two designs for the first round of testing. The initial contracts are valued at $14.5m for up to 48 drones. Colonel Danielle Medaglia, the US Army's UAS project manager, described the service's test-as-you-fly approach. "This… first tranche is going to really allow us to learn," Medaglia said. "We're going to develop those tactics, techniques and procedures, and then form programmes of instruction."

The Precision Drone Works C-100 is a quadcopter design weighing 21.4lb. It is carried in a backpack-sized container and can be assembled for flight in less than two minutes. It can fly up to 74 minutes with a payload at up to 40mph. The Anduril Ghost-X is a single rotor design similar to a miniature helicopter. It carries a 20lb payload up to 75 minutes. Both designs can operate in GPS-degraded environments. Both designs are also on the US DoD Defense Innovation Unit's Blue list of commercial systems which do not contain Chinese-made components.

LEFT: The Anduril Ghost X drone resembles a small helicopter. It has a central rail for carrying different payloads. (US ARMY)

Hypervelocity Gun Weapon System

RIGHT: An M777 howitzer fires during a night exercise at Fort Liberty, North Carolina. The use of field artillery in air defence is an innovative concept. (US ARMY)

Hypervelocity missiles figure prominently in current military thinking. Fast and capable of evading or outrunning many air defence weapons, the efforts underway to develop them are nearly as intense as the ballistic missile programs of the 1950s and 60s. As offensive hypervelocity weapons become reality, new research is also going into their potential for defensive purposes.

In July 2024, the Army Rapid Capabilities and Critical Technologies Office (RCCTO) issued a request for information on the use of hypervelocity projectiles (HVP) against aerial threats. The service envisions a new air defence weapon able to down threats such as drones, missiles, and rockets more cheaply than using expensive advanced anti-missile systems. They would also have utility against fixed wing aircraft and helicopters.

These new projectiles would move at a speed of Mach 8 or 9 and have an onboard system to communicate with sensors to guide the HVP to the incoming target. Prior to firing, the HVP would receive pre-launch information. After firing, it would manoeuvre toward its target, receiving periodic updates from the sensor systems observing that target.

This new munition is intended for use in the field artillery's 155mm cannon. A shell that size is powerful enough to easily destroy any aerial threat in existence. The army is already

BELOW: An M109A7 Paladin of 1st Battalion, 201st Field Artillery regiment prepares to fire during exercise Northern Strike 24 at Camp Grayling, Michigan. New ammunition such as the HVP makes artillery units more flexible. (US ARMY)

well-equipped with 155mm weapons, using the M777 towed and M109 Paladin self-propelled guns, and has a logistics and maintenance support system to keep them functioning. Towed guns have proven vulnerable in frontline service in Ukraine - employing them as air defence weapons may allow them to be located in less vulnerable positions. BAE Systems has a similar HVP projectile for use in the US Navy's 5in (127mm) guns, so a system using 155mm rounds is feasible.

Lieutenant General Robert Rasch, head of the RCCTO, stated the army will begin testing on the HVP in 2025. Rasch said the HVP is: "...an order of magnitude cheaper than its equivalent missile but can go really fast to close on the target." He also acknowledged the technical challenges while expressing excitement over the HVP's potential. "We have to learn through testing. There [are] different physical pressures that are put on that cannon – the amount of force required to project something at that speed," he said. "It's an impressive capability. I'm looking forward to trying to turn it into an army platform."

Army buying solar powered drone

Long endurance UAS tested in Pacific

In late 2024 and following extensive testing, the US Army ordered $20m worth of a new high endurance Unmanned Aerial System. The new K1000ULE (Ultra Long Endurance) drone is produced by Kraus Hamdani Aerospace, a relatively new company that uses onboard artificial intelligence that mimics the flight behaviours of birds to allow for quiet, efficient aerial movement.

Under the US Department of Defense guidelines for unmanned systems, the K1000ULE is a Class 2 UAS, meaning it is in the 21-55lb weight class. Class 2s generally operate below 3,500ft and have a speed of less than 250kts. This puts it in the same category as the Scan Eagle UAS in use by the US Navy and Marine Corps. A simple video game-like user interface allows a single soldier to operate multiple K1000ULEs, assigning and re-tasking them at need.

The system is solar powered, the source of its long endurance. The tops of its wings contain solar panels, allowing the UAS to recharge its batteries as it flies, vastly extending its flight time. A K1000ULE set an endurance record for class 2 UAS of 76 hours, impressive for a system that small. Electric power makes the system quieter, and its bird-like flight pattern makes it harder to detect. It also has zero emissions.

Launch is accomplished by a mount attached to a vehicle such as a lorry, rising into the air on its own as the wings get enough air beneath them. It takes about 10 minutes to assemble the UAS from its carrying case. It lands on 3-D printed skids which are simply replaced when they wear out.

This new drone will provide communications, electronic warfare and Intelligence, Surveillance and Reconnaissance (ISR) capabilities to its user. The army tested the K1000ULE during exercises in the Pacific, including Balikatan 24 in the Philippines. During the exercise, the system reconnoitred an airfield on a remote island. The type also flew data-gathering missions over the South China Sea. Most of the army's initial purchase will go to the service's multi-domain task forces: up to five of these units are planned with three currently active. Their long endurance will be useful anywhere, but especially in the vast reaches of the Pacific region. The rest of the order will go to Special Operations Command.

ABOVE: Soldiers pose with a K1000ULE during testing at Fort Irwin, California. (US ARMY)

LEFT: In a still taken from video, a K1000Ule takes off from a small automobile during testing at Aqaba, Jordan. (US NAVY)

Learning from the Ukraine War

Soldiers of the 101st Airborne Division's 2nd Brigade conducted a large scale exercise in August 2024 designed to take lessons learned from the Ukraine War and put them into practice for American troops. They began this training rotation by moving an entire brigade over 500 miles by helicopter in one night, from Fort Campbell, Kentucky, to Fort Johnson, Louisiana. Such a large, long-distance movement is difficult in itself, but the real challenge began after they arrived.

The exercise pitted the 101st against the 1st Battalion, 509th Infantry Regiment (1-509), an independent infantry unit stationed at Fort Johnson to act as an Opposing Force (OPFOR) at the Joint Readiness Training Center (JRTC). Here, combat units face this seasoned OPFOR to engage in scenarios based on real-world conflicts. Known by their nickname 'Geronimo,' 1-509, can tailor their OPFOR groups as anything from guerrilla forces to airborne or mechanised infantry with armoured support.

The 101st came prepared to try new methods based on lessons from the Ukraine War, forcing their opponents to react to the latest combat techniques. In Ukraine, electronic warfare is used extensively to detect enemy units based on their electronic signature and emissions. Unmanned Aerial Systems (UAS) are also used to locate and direct fire against opponents.

Soldiers from 101st used large numbers of small Raspberry Pi computers, a single board design slightly larger than a credit card, which can be purchased easily on sites such as Amazon. These devices were used to simulate the electronic signature of computers and other electronic devices and confuse the soldiers of 1-509, who were actively searching for such emissions to locate headquarters and communications nodes.

The 101st instituted a 'deception plan,' designed to make it appear

as though the 2nd Brigade was in a different position from its actual locations so their enemy "...would commit forces into our strongest defences and not into our weakest," according to Captain Charlie O'Hagan, commanding a Multi-Functional Reconnaissance Company (MFRC) in the 101st. On the first two nights of the exercise one battalion would turn on its decoys to make it appear they were moving in a false direction.

The plan achieved some success as the OPFOR deployed Intelligence, Surveillance and Reconnaissance (ISR) assets against the decoys, as well as some artillery support. O'Hagan continued: "Ideally, they'll use something in terms of artillery to destroy the decoy, which means the enemy unmasks his artillery. We can pick up on it, and then we can counter-fire his artillery."

Although this was a setback to 1-509's OPFOR group in this exercise, they train a different brigade nearly every month. Any lesson they learn in the current exercise is incorporated for use in the next exercise, enabling constant improvement. The exercise also showed the importance of frequent movement to prevent being spotted. One OPFOR unit suffered an attack when it stayed in place too long and a UAS from the 101st MFRC found them.

Lt Col Mason Thornal, commanding the OPFOR, noted the 101st had more ISR and strike assets than normal and altered his procedures to compensate. "When we were infiltrating the area of operations," he said, "...We had to serialise our movements so instead of sending eight tanks at once – two here, two here, two here – it made us much slower."

Both sides gained new understanding of the importance of movement, concealment and camouflage and of moving quietly in smaller elements, coming together only when necessary for a massed blow to the enemy. This minimised the chances of being detected by UAS, while putting out no electronic signature kept opponents from determining the size of a given force. Anything that can be detected can be engaged with artillery, attack helicopters, or can simply be jammed.

Before beginning a mission, soldiers are inspected to make sure they aren't carrying anything which can emit an electronic signature, such as a mobile phone or smart watch. One report noted even electric shavers must be turned off to avoid detection.

The exercise also identified that headquarters units, which in the past have tended to be large and slow to move, must also become smaller and mobile. If a UAS spots a large concentration of command tents, vehicles and antennae, its location will quickly come under fire, destroying it or forcing it to move so its loses control of its subordinate units.

LEFT: Soldiers of 2nd Brigade disembark from a CH-47 Chinook helicopter after a 500-mile movement at the beginning of the exercise. (US ARMY)

BOTTOM: A gunner from 1-509 uses his M240 machine gun to lay a base of fire so the rest of his squad can manoeuvre during a night attack. (US ARMY)

BELOW: Soldiers prepare to move out in an Infantry Squad Vehicle that has just been delivered by a helicopter. (US ARMY)

Multinational Arctic Exercises

11th Airborne Division tests itself and allies

Expanded interest and concerns about the arctic region has brought renewed interest in training there for the US Army. In February 2024 a large-scale exercise by the Joint Pacific Multinational Readiness Center (JPMRC) brought over 8,000 troops from three countries together for advanced training.

Soldiers from the relatively new 11th Airborne Division joined troops from the 3rd Battalion, Princess Patricia's Canadian Light Infantry, and the Royal Canadian Air Force, along with an infantry company from Mongolia. South Korea, Sweden, and Finland also sent staff sections to work with US headquarters units to improve interoperability and understanding, particularly from the two new NATO members. Other nations sent observers.

This is the third year the JPMRC has conducted Arctic warfare training exercises in Alaska and this iteration was the largest and most ambitious yet. One US Army priority is to improve its capabilities in the Arctic region, in response to Russian and

Chinese militarization of the Arctic in the last decade.

During the exercise two battalions of the division's 2nd Brigade acted as the enemy force for its 1st Brigade. To give their opponents a real challenge, the 2nd Brigade was given large amounts of rocket and artillery ammunition (simulated, of course) as well as equipment for electronic warfare, communications jamming and air defence. This firepower advantage forced the 1st Brigade to innovate, rapidly find and strike targets and move quickly to avoid enemy artillery.

It also meant friendly forces had to fight to control the air over the simulated battlefield. The division's Apache attack helicopters carried out a 150-mile deep attack by flying low to the ground and weaving through hilly terrain to reach their targets undetected. Other troops made an air assault after moving 80 miles.

On the ground, troops tested five new Cold-Weather, All-Terrain Vehicles (CATV), recently delivered under contract from BAE Systems. This new vehicle can carry nine soldiers and their equipment. 'Enemy' forces used small drones to locate their opponents and armed them with tennis balls and footballs as simulated ordnance, a lesson from Ukraine. A HIMARS rocket launcher was flown over 500 miles to the far northern city of Utqiagvik, above the Arctic circle for a surprise fire mission.

The exercise showed needs for improvement as well, including better tents and ski bindings. Commanders also learned the unit needs better methods of casualty evacuation and more snowmobiles for better mobility.

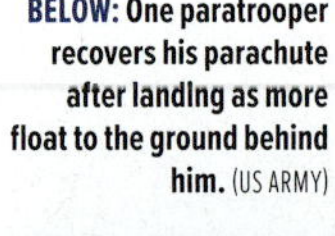

Sniper Competition

A contest between elite sniper teams

In March 2024 the US Army John F Kennedy Special Warfare Center and School hosted the US Army Special Operations Command International Best Sniper Competition at Fort Liberty, North Carolina. This is the contest's 15th year, a four-day event with 23 stages designed to test each sniper team's skill under simulated combat conditions. Each stage was based on real-world sniper missions.

Instructors at the US Army Special Forces Sniper Course designed the ranges which stressed long-range marksmanship and sniper tactics. Each three-person sniper team worked cooperatively to simply get through the competition, much less win. Each event required them to engage different kinds of targets, such as personnel or vehicles, stationary and moving, at different distances, including events with time limitations.

To increase the stress on the competitors, prior to the event they do not see the area where the event will take place. They were loaded in a van just before the event, taken to its location and given a small book describing what they must do. Five minutes later they began the course. Some events further stressed the competitors by requiring them to pull weighted sleds or do other physical activity to increase their heart rates and respiration.

While the events showcased each sniper's ability with their primary weapon, their rifle, many events also required them to use backup weapons such as pistols. This might simulate a sniper being discovered after making a long-range shot and then having to engage enemy troops who are hunting for them. Sniper rifles excel at long distance shooting but are not ideal for close quarters combat.

US Army 1st Sgt Lin of the 1st Special Forces Group (SFG) described the sniper's craft. "Shooting is probably only ten percent of the job," he said. "A lot of it is reconnaissance, a lot of it is physical fitness, a lot of rehearsals." Often, all of a sniper team's skills in scouting, stealth, and movement are needed to get into a position to place a single well-aimed shot at a critical place.

Army representation included teams from the 1st, 3rd, 5th, 7th, 10th, and 19th SFGs and 75th Ranger Regiment. Sniper teams from the US Marine Corps, US Navy Special Warfare Group and US Coast Guard also participated. Six allied nations - Belgium, France, Germany, Ireland, Italy, and the Netherlands also sent teams.

The team from the 3rd SFG won the competition, getting bragging rights within the special operations community. Second place went to France with the 10th SFG in third place.

ABOVE: A sniper engages stationary and moving targets on a range during the competition. (US ARMY)

LEFT: A cartridge case flies from the ejection port of a sniper's rifle during an event. (US ARMY)

Super Garuda Shield 24

Pacific exercise grows in scope

RIGHT: A machine gunner from the 25th Infantry Division takes aim. (US ARMY)

The Super Garuda Shield series are among the most important readiness and training exercises for the US Army in the Pacific region. They are hosted by Indonesia and held in that nation. The first Garuda Shield occurred in 2007 as a bilateral exercise between the US and Indonesia. Since then, it has grown into the Super Garuda Shield, held annually for the last three years and involving multiple countries.

As the political and military situation in the Pacific region has evolved and become more complex, the exercise has adapted and grown to incorporate many allied and partner nations from around the world. The 2024 exercise ran from August 26 to September 6 in East Java. Participating nations included Indonesia, the United States, Japan, Singapore, the United Kingdom, Australia, Canada, France, Brazil, Brunei, India, South Korea, New Zealand, and Thailand.

Any conflict in the region will involve land, sea, air, cyber and space forces acting in concert. This year the US Army formed a Joint Operations Center (JOC) to coordinate forces from not only different branches of service but different nations. A sub-exercise, name Joint Strike, combined intelligence assets from the US Army, US Navy and Indonesian military to rapidly locate and engage targets using forces all three entities.

US Army Brig Gen Kevin Williams, the deputy commander for operations for the 25th Infantry Division, acted as the army forces commander for the overall exercise. Williams said: "Deploying an entire task force under an army forces command structure, integrating forces by ship and air, and coordinating across joint services, including the navy, Marine Corps, and air force, are significant undertakings. But these challenges present invaluable opportunities to build a coalition, exercise under realistic conditions, and enhance our collective readiness. The participation of over 23 nations and the full spectrum of US and Indonesian joint forces demonstrates our commitment to enhancing readiness, improving warfighting skills, and fostering interoperability across the multinational spectrum."

The 25th Infantry Division is the US Army's primary combat force for the Pacific. Its units frequently take part in exercises and deployments across the region. Over time the division has developed extensive understanding of the cultural, political and military nuances of the nations which make up the area. The relatively new 11th Airborne Division also took part in the exercise, increasing its own knowledge and relationships. The exercise also sees US troops engage in engineering and medical projects which help local populations.

BELOW: American and Indonesian soldiers disembark from helicopters during an air assault mission. (US ARMY)

Defender 24

Moving to Europe, ready to fight

Defending Europe effectively against a Russian attack is a major priority for the US Army. Currently the chances of a Russian invasion of NATO territory are lower, as Russia is thoroughly engaged in fighting in Ukraine. However, if the Russians ultimately succeed in Ukraine, they may be emboldened to act elsewhere against NATO's periphery, such as in the Baltic states, Eastern Europe, or the long, shared border with new NATO members Finland and Sweden. NATO wishes to convince its adversaries of the futility of such aggression.

While the United States has committed additional forces to Europe since the Ukraine War began, in the event of war more troops from the United States would be quickly moved to the continent. There, they would be issued weapons and equipment from the prepositioned stocks the United States keeps in several locations across Europe and immediately move into action alongside NATO troops from other nations.

Exercise Defender 24, held from March 28 to May 31, 2024, practiced exactly those contingencies for the US Army. The 2024 iteration was one of NATO's largest exercises in decades, involving 17,000 American and 23,000 military personnel from 22 NATO members and partner nations. The exercise incorporated three sub-exercises:

Saber Strike: This monthlong event involved the US 2nd Cavalry Regiment (organised as a Stryker Brigade Combat Team) and V Corps, along with German troops from 21st Panzer Brigade, Italians of the 8th Bersaglieri Regiment, and Spanish soldiers of the Brigade Galicia, among others. The exercise placed focus on command and control between allied nations.

Immediate Response: Taking place in the Czech Republic, this exercise placed both active and reserve components of the US Army alongside Czech troops of their 7th Mechanised Brigade. A headquarters element of the Virginia National Guard's 29th Infantry Division led the exercise, which also involved National Guard troops from West Virginia and Kentucky. The training included live fire exercises.

Swift Response: Spread across Germany, Romania and Sweden, this portion of Defender 24 focused on a rapid response to an invasion of NATO territory using airborne forces. Several thousand paratroopers made jumps during the exercise, including troops from the 82nd Airborne Division. There were also helicopter air assaults and live fire training events. A 155mm Paladin-equipped artillery battalion from the Georgia National Guard deployed to Sweden, firing missions for Swedish Army units.

Repelling any invasion of NATO territory will require cooperation from multiple member nations. Exercises such as this foster the familiarity and partnership needed to succeed in a shooting war.

ABOVE: A US multi-role bridging company uses a ferry to transport two British Army Warrior infantry fighting vehicles across a river in Poland. (US ARMY)

LEFT: A Stryker Dragoon armoured vehicle moves past a fire team during a live fire exercise in Poland during Defender 24. (US ARMY)

Rescue at Los Banos

RIGHT: Lieutenant General Robert Eichelberger, commanding US 8th Army and Major General Joseph Swing commanding 11th Airborne Division confer over a map prior to the raid. (US ARMY)

When the Japanese captured the Philippine Islands in early 1942, they rounded up thousands of American citizens living there and placed them into internment camps. Their treatment by the occupying Japanese steadily deteriorated in the following years, with disease and hunger debilitating and sometimes killing the captives. When the Americans invaded the Philippines in late 1944 to recapture them from the Japanese, the situation in the internment camps grew severe. Concern arose that the Japanese would execute their prisoners.

An intelligence officer in the 11th Airborne Division learned of the existence of over 2,100 American prisoners at Los Banos, an old agricultural college south of Manila. It was within striking distance for an airborne force, so he began gathering information for a possible rescue attempt. The camp had a guard force of 150-250 troops and there were Japanese units stationed nearby. On February 19, 1945, three escaped prisoners reached the 11th Airborne headquarters and provided details of the layout of the camp, including its defences. Two officers covertly reached the camp and examined it, picking out drop zones for the paratroopers. A lake sat just north of the camp and the Americans held the far shore.

The plan was risky, but daring, involving three elements. First a company of paratroopers, B Company of the 511th Parachute Infantry Regiment, would land next to the camp and seize it, assisted by local Filipino guerrillas. Second, A and C companies would cross the lake in amphibious tractors (Amtracs),

RIGHT: An Amtrac loaded with civilian internees leaves the Los Banos camp during the evacuation. (US ARMY)

occupy the villages along the shoreline and hold the area while the civilians were loaded on the Amtracs for evacuation across the lake. Third, a battalion-sized group named Task Force Soule would approach the area over land, providing a diversion to the Japanese. If the Japanese began killing the prisoners, the guerillas would attack immediately.

BELOW: Pack howitzers of the 675th Parachute Field Artillery Regiment fire their guns in the Philippines. This unit supported the raiding force during the liberation of the Los Banos camp. (US ARMY)

with green smoke grenades, which the pilots quickly spotted and other scouts used green smoke to direct the Amtracs onto shore.

The paratroopers jumped at 6:58am, just as the scout groups attacked the camp perimeter. As the paratroopers floated to the ground, the scouts opened fire. One group of four guards died in a single long burst from a Browning Automatic Rifle (BAR). Some Japanese fled, but guerrillas chased them down and the group assigned to the main gate came in so fast they kept going through the gate and seized the camp armoury, shooting any Japanese they found.

The paratroopers formed platoons and went straight into an attack. They took machine gun fire from the camp perimeter but quickly silenced the enemy weapons. Some guards took cover in a bunker near the main gate, so the Americans destroyed it with grenades and 60mm mortars. Guards who fled into the jungles were met by guerrillas with machetes and bolo knives. American paratroopers gunned down the guards who tried to hide among the internees, most of whom took cover when the shooting started.

Resistance soon ended and the paratroopers began organising the civilians for evacuation. The internees were starving and many weighed less than 100lb (seven stones or 45kg); the fit paratroopers towered over them. Some hid, fearful the Japanese would return. The Amtracs drove up to the camp, but there were not enough to carry everyone in one trip. They left with one load of civilians while the rest stayed on the beach, protected by the paratroopers. At 1pm the Amtracs returned and picked up the rest of the civilians and rescue force. By 4pm the internees were all together again, eating their first meal as free people in three years.

Planning for the operation occurred simultaneously with the intelligence gathering efforts. This happened so quickly that few written orders were issued, and the paratroopers adapted as new information appeared. The actual written orders were completed later purely for historical documentation.

On February 21-22, a platoon of reconnaissance troops infiltrated the area of the camp and rendezvoused with the guerrillas. These troops split into small teams, each with a squad of guerrillas. One team secured the landing zone and stood ready to mark it with green smoke when the planes appeared overhead. Another team secured the beach where the Amtracs would come ashore. Other teams would attack the guards manning the main gate and guard towers.

The Japanese detected many of the American preparations but drew the wrong conclusions. They misidentified Task Force Soule as the main effort and focused all their effort against it. The Japanese did not seem to consider so much effort would be directed at rescuing civilians. The camp guards had no idea what was coming.

At 4am on February 23, soldiers boarded the Amtracs and in an hour were on their way. As they approached their landing beach just over another hour later, they saw the nine C-47 transports carrying B Company. The recce platoon marked the drop zone

BELOW: Paratroopers of the 511th PIR put on their equipment before a parachute jump in the Philippines. (US ARMY)

Operation Eagle Claw

Disaster in the Iranian desert

ABOVE: A sufficient number of large transport helicopters were critical to the success of the operation. After several were lost to mechanical breakdown, the mission could not go forward. *(US NAVY)*

Two days after the newly formed Delta Force passed its final validation exercises to become operational, it received its first mission. On November 4, 1979, revolutionary students in Iran attacked and seized the United States Embassy in Tehran, taking the staff hostage. Planning for a possible rescue mission began immediately, alongside diplomatic efforts. Delta's leader, Colonel Charles Beckwith, did much of the planning.

To gather intelligence for the mission, soon named Operation Eagle Claw, both the army and Central Intelligence Agency (CIA) sent operatives into Tehran. One was a special forces soldier and the other an air force member, both of whom had grown up in Iran. A few operators from the Berlin Special Forces Detachment also went posing as German businessmen. They were highly skilled in covert operations in urban settings.

It was believed that most of the 53 hostages were being held on the embassy grounds, though three who were not present when the embassy was taken were held at the Ministry of Foreign Affairs. The Berlin Special Forces men did their job so well that several gained entry to the ministry building while another got photographs of the students at the embassy.

The final plan called for a two-day operation. On the first night six C-130s would carry the rescue force and supplies, including 6,000 gallons of fuel, to a remote site code-named Desert One. A small force of US Army Rangers would secure the site. Meanwhile eight US Navy RH-53D Sea Stallion helicopters would fly from the carrier USS *Nimitz* in the Persian Gulf and land at Desert One. A minimum of six were required for the mission.

After refuelling, the helicopters would carry the Delta Force operators 260 miles to a second site called Desert Two, only 52 miles

RIGHT: Delta Force operatives boarding the aircraft that would take them to the staging base for the operation. The man facing the camera has a CAR-15 carbine; also visible are an M3 submachine gun and a shotgun. The team had wide latitude to pick their weapons. *(US DoD)*

As the smugglers tried to escape a Ranger hit the truck with a rocket launcher, causing a large explosion. The truck's driver jumped into the lorry and escaped. A few minutes later a bus carrying 44 civilians also appeared. The Rangers disabled it and took the civilians prisoner until the operation ended.

The helicopters also ran into bad luck. One suffered a mechanical breakdown and had to land in the desert. It was abandoned after the crew was picked up. The rest of the helicopters ran into a haboob, a dust storm local to the area, which forced another helicopter to return to the *Nimitz*. The remaining six arrived at Desert One, but one had a malfunctioning hydraulic system.

This brought the number of available helicopters to less than needed to complete the mission. After heated discussions, Beckwith, and other leaders at Desert One reported their situation via satellite phone and were ordered to abort.

To refuel all the aircraft for the return flights, one of the helicopters had to be moved. As it did so it drifted in the dust cloud created by its rotors and crashed into a C-130, causing a massive explosion and fire. Eight aircrew died in the accident and the remaining force had to quickly withdraw.

The mission ended in failure. Some of the force withdrew back to Masirah. Despite security precautions, some RAF personnel at the base guessed at the mission's purpose and sent two cases of beer with a message: "To you from all of us for having the guts to try."

It was not a good beginning for Delta Force, but the lessons learned led to vast improvements in American special operations and joint operations capabilities. The highly capable US Special Operations Command (SOCOM) was born from this disaster in the desert.

LEFT: A grainy image of the wreckage of the destroyed C-130 in the Iranian desert. During the evacuation equipment and weapons were left behind. (US DoD)

LEFT: An unfortunately blurry image of US Army Rangers training for Operation Eagle Claw. Their mission was to secure the landing fields while the Delta operatives conducted the hostage rescue. (US ARMY)

BELOW: Colonel Charles Beckwith led the US Army contingent for the operation. He retired shortly after the operation.

from Tehran. There, they would camouflage the helicopters and hide until the next nightfall. That evening, CIA operatives would bring trucks to Desert Two and pick up the rescue force, driving them to the city where they would rendezvous with the CIA and special forces assets already there. These assets would guide the rescue force to the embassy and ministry. While they were en route, other US forces would knock out the electrical grid to confuse and delay any Iranian response. Air support was available from US Navy carrier aircraft and USAF AC-130 gunships.

The Delta operatives were subdivided into several elements to affect the rescue, provide covering fire and block any responding Iranian forces. The assault team included 120 Delta personnel. After eliminating the guards and rescuing the hostages, the entire force would move to a nearby football stadium where the helicopters would pick them up. A few mile outside Tehran was the Manzariyeh Air Base. The plan was that a company of Rangers would capture this base so that USAF C-141 transports could land and evacuate the entire group to safety.

The actual mission began on April 24, 1980. The C-130s took off from a staging base on Masirah Island near Oman and landed at Desert One with one aircraft suffering damage but remaining flyable. However, as the Americans began to secure the area, a tanker truck and a lorry appeared, driven by fuel smugglers.

Operation Urgent Fury

In the early 1980s, the small island nation of Grenada in the Caribbean descended into chaos as competing factions fought for control. On October 19, 1983, the country's socialist Prime Minister, Maurice Bishop, popular with the populace and allied to communist Cuba, was gunned down in the street by a faction of the Grenadian People's Revolutionary Army (GPRA). About 800 American citizens lived in Grenada, 600 of them medical students, and their fate became the stated reason that the United States took interest in the situation, launching a rescue mission on October 25.

Other reasons also influenced the American decision. An airport under construction at the island's southwest tip involved Cuban troops and workers. In 1983, the US began stationing Pershing II missiles in Germany and leaders were concerned that the Soviets might be planning to base SS-20 missiles on the island. Landing troops on the island would show American determination without a direct confrontation. Rescuing the students was a legitimate concern, but not the only one.

The plan for the landing quickly expanded to involve all four military branches including the US Army. The army's contribution included the 75th Ranger Regiment, paratroopers from the 82nd Airborne Division, and a team from Delta Force. The Rangers would land at the airport, disembark, and secure it. Paratroopers would land later and take over security of the site while the Rangers advanced to the nearby True Blue Medical Campus and rescued the students. Other Rangers were to capture the GPRA's main base.

Meanwhile, five US Army MH-60 Blackhawk helicopters would land Delta and some Rangers at the island's Richmond Hill Prison to free political prisoners. The US Marine Corps and Navy SEALs had other objectives alongside the army. These included seizing the island radio station and rescuing the British-appointed governor general, Sir Paul Scoon.

Expected opposition included the GPRA, with up to 1,200 regular troops and between 2,000 and 5,000 militia. In the event, only a fraction of these numbers actively resisted. There were almost 800 Cubans on the island, but less than 100 were active military personnel. Most were construction workers, though they were also military reservists. After the American arrived, the ranking Cuban officer issued weapons to them, claiming self-defence as the reason and this clouded the status of the Cubans later.

The Rangers boarded their C-130 transport at midnight on October 24. While en route they learned that the runway at the airport was obstructed, so they changed the plan to a parachute landing. The drop began at 05:30am on October 25. The Rangers took ground fire during the assault from both 23mm anti-aircraft

guns and BTR-60 armoured vehicles. Once on the ground, the US troops knocked out the BTRs with recoilless rifles and the help of an AC-130 gunship. They next used captured construction equipment to clear the runway and by 10am reinforcements were landing by aircraft.

Two hours after the parachute landing, a company of Rangers moved to the True Blue medical campus and drove off a small GPRA force. However, the American students they discovered told them over half their number was at a second campus at Grand Anse, two miles away.

Concerned an overland advance would cause the GPRA and Cubans to occupy that campus, the next day Marine helicopters were used to lift the Rangers to Grand Anse, who took the campus after a short fight.

A second helicopter assault against a GPRA barracks occurred on the third day, October 27. That barracks turned out to be empty, but three Rangers died and four were wounded in a helicopter crash. The Delta Force mission failed to take the prison due to bad intelligence, though it did capture a few important prisoners. The paratroopers also fought skirmishes with the GPRA and Cubans, but by the end of the day the fighting was essentially over.

The operation, though a success overall, pointed out serious shortcomings in intelligence collection, coordination, planning and joint force operations. For example, the Marine commander of the helicopter unit which carried the Rangers into Grand Anse initially refused to transport army personnel. He relented only when threatened with court martial. One assessment stated most of the 25 Americans killed in the operation were lost due to mistakes and intelligence failures.

Though the operation received both domestic and international criticism, it proved popular with the American populace, happy to see a success after the failed Operation Eagle Claw. The true legacy for the US military came through the lessons learned and the subsequent passing of the Goldwater-Nichols Department of Defense Reorganization Act of 1986, which put US forces on the path to better professionalism and unified joint operations.

LEFT: Paratroopers take cover behind an embankment during a patrol. Several US patrols were attacked by Cuban and Grenadian troops during the operation. (US ARMY)

LEFT: Paratroopers firing M102 105mm howitzers. Poor maps hindered US artillery's effectiveness during the operation. (US ARMY)

BELOW: Rangers of Company C, 1st Battalion advance. Rangers continued to wear the olive drab uniform after the rest of the army switched to then-new camouflage clothing. They also often wore the 'patrol cap' instead of helmets. (US DoD)

Operation Kayla Mueller

The death of Abu Bakr Al-Baghdadi

Abu Bakr al-Baghdadi acted as an insurgent for many years in Iraq before he rose to lead the so-called Islamic State (IS) in Iraq and Syria. Exactly when and where he became radicalised is a matter of debate, but he helped create a militant group in Iraq after the 2003 invasion. His arrest in February 2004 by US forces led to his detainment until December of that year. From that point he gradually rose in prominence in the Islamic State of Iraq group until, as its leader, he announced the creation of IS in April 2013.

During his time as leader, al-Baghdadi kept a number of women as slaves. One of them was American citizen Kayla Mueller, an aid worker captured by IS in Aleppo, Syria in August 2013. She soon became a personal captive of al-Baghdadi and during her time as an IS prisoner she suffered frequent sexual assault, abuse, and torture. IS released two differing accounts of her death in February 2015, stating she died as a result of either a Jordanian or American airstrike. There are disputes with this claim, including that she may have been killed on al-Baghdadi's orders. The true circumstances of her death remain unclear.

US and allied forces continued their campaign against IS, mainly through support of local forces, enabling them to gradually defeat IS and retake the territory it had captured. This coalition effectively destroyed IS as an organised force at the Battle of Baghuz Fawqani in February 2019, although disorganised remnants still exist. US Special Operations Forces (SOF) saw wide service in this conflict, as did US airpower.

Al-Baghdadi did not remain with his fighters but rather went into hiding. The hunt for him continued until October 2019, when sufficient evidence was gathered to pinpoint his location to a compound near Barisha, Syria. The effort involved America's CIA and intelligence agencies from Iraq, Turkey, Kurdish and Syrian Democratic Forces. Reportedly, an IS fighter also turned informant for the Kurds, providing vital information about the compound, including the presence of a tunnel network at the site.

The SOF assigned to the mission named it Operation Kayla Mueller, further calling their group Task Force 8-14, for the month and day of Mueller's birthday. The operation began on October 26, 2019. It included A Squadron of the 1st Special Forces Operational Detachment – Delta, the 160th Special Operations Aviation Regiment, and the 75th Ranger Regiment.

Drones kept the compound under observation as the assault force moved there. Both jet attack aircraft and armed helicopters were stationed to quickly provide close air support if needed. However, as there were believed to be children and other non-combatants in the home, efforts were made to minimise casualties.

As the assault force approached in MH-47 Chinook and MH-60 Blackhawk

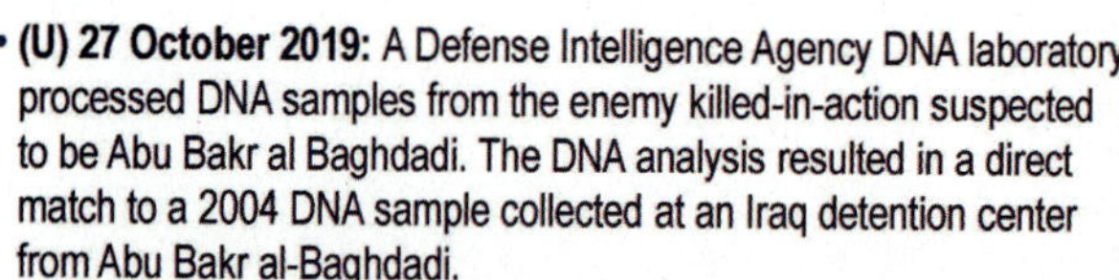

(U) THE POSITIVE IDENTIFICATION OF ABU BAKR AL-BAGHDADI

- **(U) 27 October 2019:** A Defense Intelligence Agency DNA laboratory processed DNA samples from the enemy killed-in-action suspected to be Abu Bakr al Baghdadi. The DNA analysis resulted in a direct match to a 2004 DNA sample collected at an Iraq detention center from Abu Bakr al-Baghdadi.

  - Statistical analysis indicates a probability of **1 in 104 Septillion** (1.04×10^{26}) to support this match.

- **(U)** For perspective, if the population of earth was 14.8 quadrillion times what it is today (~7 billion), you would still only expect to find one person with this DNA profile.

helicopters, they took fire from local militants outside the compound. The supporting armed helicopters silenced the militants with cannon fire. And the transport helicopters, carrying between 50 and 70 Delta operators and Rangers, landed outside the compound's wall. The Rangers quickly formed a cordon around the site and cleared several tents near the compound. The Delta operators, using Arabic, called on the occupants to surrender and come out. A number of people, including children, came out without resistance and were taken prisoner, though later released.

The Delta operators believed the entrance was rigged with explosives, so they blew a hole in the wall to gain entry. During this time five militants were killed and two more captured; several of those killed wore suicide vests. Delta quickly entered the house and discovered Baghdadi had fled into the tunnels below, taking two young children with him. Conan, a military working dog with 50 missions to his credit, followed by a bomb disposal robot, went into the tunnel after him.

Baghdadi reached a dead end and decided to detonate the suicide vest he wore, killing himself and both children. The tunnel partially collapsed, and Conan was wounded. Operators went into the tunnel, found Conan, dug out Baghdadi's body and used DNA sampling to confirm his identity. Afterward, they searched the compound for documents and other items of intelligence value before departing the area about two hours after they landed. The strike aircraft destroyed the site with bombs and missiles to prevent its use as a shrine.

Operation Kayla Mueller stands as an example of the professionalism of American SOF and the ability of the US military to carry out joint operations. It shows how far the army's Delta Force has evolved since Operation Eagle Claw, almost 40 years earlier.

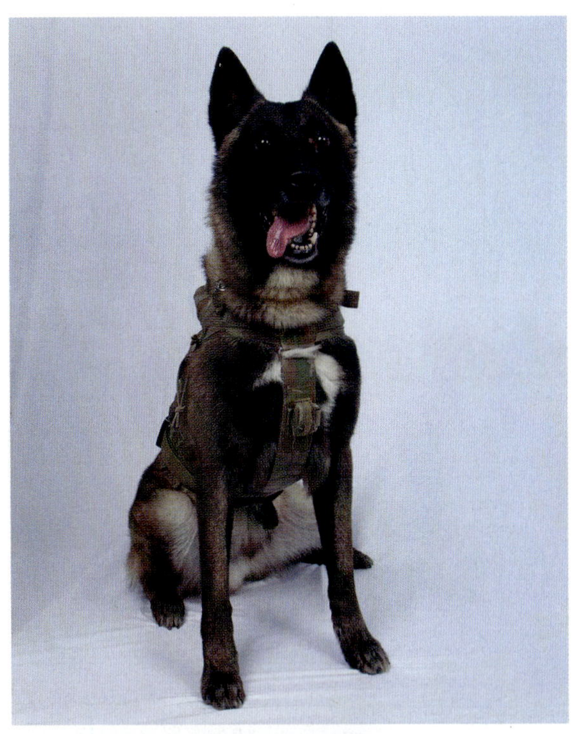

ABOVE: Conan, the Belgian Malinois who chased down al-Baghdadi during the raid. He recovered from his injuries and returned to duty, dying of cancer in 2023. (US DoD)

LEFT: At lower right, US special operations troops approach al-Baghdadi's compound. (US DoD)

LEFT: A drone observes and records the compound before the raid. The operation had extensive air support, isolating the compound from any possible IS support. (US DoD)

The Combat Applications Group

The US Army's top special forces unit is the 1st Special Forces Operational Detachment – Delta (1st SFOD-D). They are known by several nicknames, including The Unit and Task Force Green but are best known as Delta Force. Within the US military they are frequently referred to as the Combat Applications Group (CAG). Whatever name is applied to them, this highly secretive group is the most elite of the US Army's already selective Special Operations Forces (SOF). It specialises in counterterrorism, unconventional operations, hostage rescue, intelligence gathering and surveillance.

SFOD-D falls under the operational control of Joint Special Operations Command (JSOC). This command oversees high-level SOF from across the US military. Further, JSOC is a subordinate command of Special Operations Command (SOCCOM), which itself oversees all SOF in the US military. While this is a somewhat complicated command arrangement, the US military has spent the last several decades practicing joint operations, to the point where it is capable of mixing forces from different service branches and using them effectively.

Delta's origins begin in the 1970s, when the proliferation of terrorism and low-intensity conflicts made the US realise it needed a military force to handle such challenges. The US Department of Defense (DoD) accepted a plan put forth by army Colonel Charles Beckwith. He was a Green Beret with extensive combat experience in Vietnam. Prior to that, he served as an exchange officer with the UK's Special Air Service (SAS), including a tour with them during the Malaya Emergency.

Beckwith was impressed by the capabilities of the SAS and advocated

ABOVE: Darkness is the operator's ally and like all special operations forces, SFOD-D train extensively to carry out missions at night. (US ARMY)

RIGHT: Seen through a night-vision device, SOF soldiers carry out a nighttime combat marksmanship course. (US ARMY)

for a similar unit within US special forces. On November 19, 1977, he received orders to create such a force within two years. Five months later he had an initial group of selectees for training. These men went through an intensive regimen of physical and mental testing where only the best of an already elite group was accepted. These men went to Fort Bragg, North Carolina (now Fort Liberty), the unit's new home.

There, the new Delta troopers learned every skill Beckwith could conceive including marksmanship, close-quarters combat, first aid, navigation, and covert operations. They even learned how to hot-wire cars and pick locks, anything that might be needed in the field. A shoot-house, common today but a new idea then, allowed them to practice rescue operations, often with one of the Delta members sitting among the practice targets as his teammates burst in and shot those targets with live ammunition. This was something SAS also did, to reinforce accuracy when rescuing hostages. Like the SAS, they also trained with civilian law enforcement agencies to learn their special skills.

In early November 1979, almost at the two-year mark, Delta performed a validation exercise which included a simultaneous assault on a building and an airplane. The exercise proved a success and Delta Force was now operational. The next day, it got its first mission when the US Embassy in Tehran, Iran, was seized by revolutionaries. This led to Operation Eagle Claw (see page 42). That mission ended in failure and tragedy due to a crash and several aircraft losses.

Despite this setback, SFOD-D went on to become a world-class SOF unit and has seen action in numerous conflicts since. This includes the 1991 Gulf War, operations in Somalia, the wars in Afghanistan and Iraq, and the campaign against the so-called Islamic State, to name a few.

Little is known about SFOD-D and often even published information is later found to be erroneous, either fictional, simply mistaken or perhaps even intentional misdirection. Even the photographs in this section are representative, as actual images of Delta Operators are rare. This is to be expected for a unit which depends on secrecy for survival and success. Recruiting standards are high; enlisted soldiers must be at the equivalent rank of corporal through master sergeant, while officers must be captains or majors. High intelligence, a clean service record and airborne training are desired as well.

Candidates must pass a physical fitness test and a series of difficult land navigation exercises. Afterward they go through psychological testing designed to observe their ability to cope with extreme pressure. If they succeed at all of that, they must still pass the Operator's Training Course. Only then will they pass into one the SFOD-D's active squadrons and begin their career as an operator.

Like any SOF unit, when not on an operation they are training constantly, honing existing skills and developing new ones. They work frequently with the SAS and other SOF units from around the world.

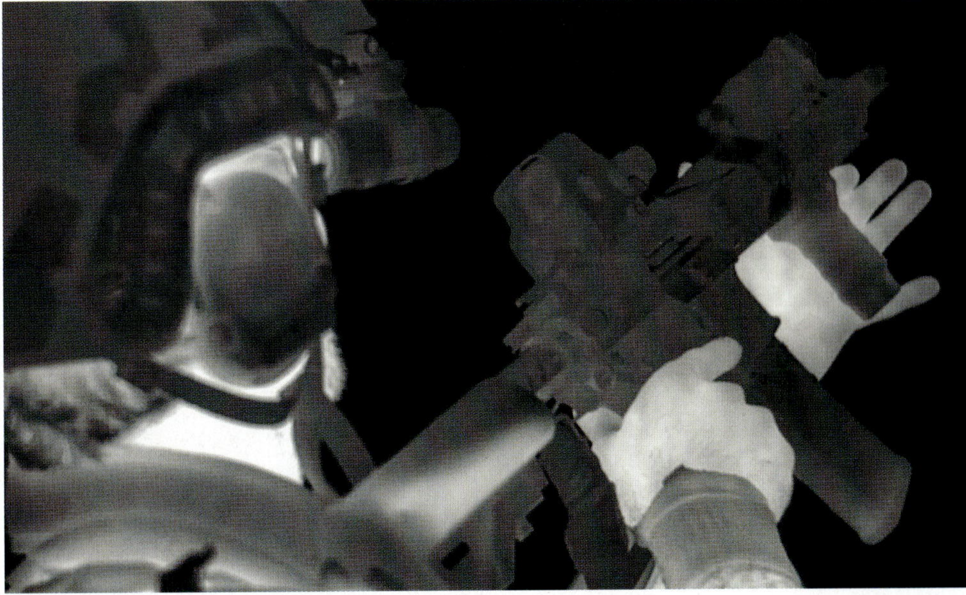

ABOVE: This view through a thermal imaging device shows a SOF operator during direct-action training in Lithuania with NATO partners. (US NAVY)

BELOW: SFOD-D adopted the 'shoot house' concept from the UK's SAS. It is now a common training tool throughout the army. (US ARMY)

75th Ranger Regiment

The 75th Ranger Regiment is the third direct action fighting element of the US Army's Special Operations Command (USASOC), after SFOD-D and the Special Forces Groups (SFG). While those two components are highly capable of nearly any mission assigned to them, both are limited in size, specific in organisation, and are very specialised. The Rangers are organised as a conventional light infantry force with special capabilities and capable of larger-scale operations than either of the other components.

The Rangers act as USASOC's raiding force, conducting quick surprise attacks. The US Army defines a raid as a surprise attack against an enemy position for a reason other than capturing or holding it. A raid focuses on a specific purpose, such as destroying the position, killing, or capturing the enemy troops occupying it, or destroying some equipment vital to the enemy. The raiding force stays there just long enough to accomplish its goal and then withdraws.

Raids have been a primary Ranger mission since the first modern Ranger units were formed during World War Two. Rangers are also well-practiced at other missions such as seizing airfields, infiltration, and long-range patrols and capturing high value targets such as enemy leaders.

The regiment is organised similarly to a light infantry BCT, though it lacks dedicated artillery or engineer support. To compensate, battalion mortar platoons are trained to use the larger 120mm mortar along with the smaller 60mm and 81mm weapons, and Ranger infantry train in many basic combat engineer skills such as the use of explosives and portable breaching equipment.

A regimental headquarters company plans and oversees the entire unit's training and operations. Unlike standard infantry BCTs, the 75th has a Military Intelligence (MI) battalion which has extended capabilities in cyber and electronic warfare. This is largely due to its role in USASOC, and to the special missions it must carry out. There is also a special troops battalion with a communications company for increased signals capability and a Selection and Training Company which oversees the Ranger School. It also contains the Regimental Reconnaissance Company (RRC), highly trained and experienced in advanced scouting techniques. This asset is frequently used by USASOC.

The heart of the regiment is its three Ranger battalions, each with six companies. A headquarters company commands the battalion. Three rifle companies, A, B, and C contain the battalion's infantry. Delta Company has the battalion's specialised assets, such as scouts, heavy mortars, Reconnaissance, Surveillance and Target Acquisition (RSTA) teams, snipers, and military working dogs. Echo Company is the battalion's support element. Regimental

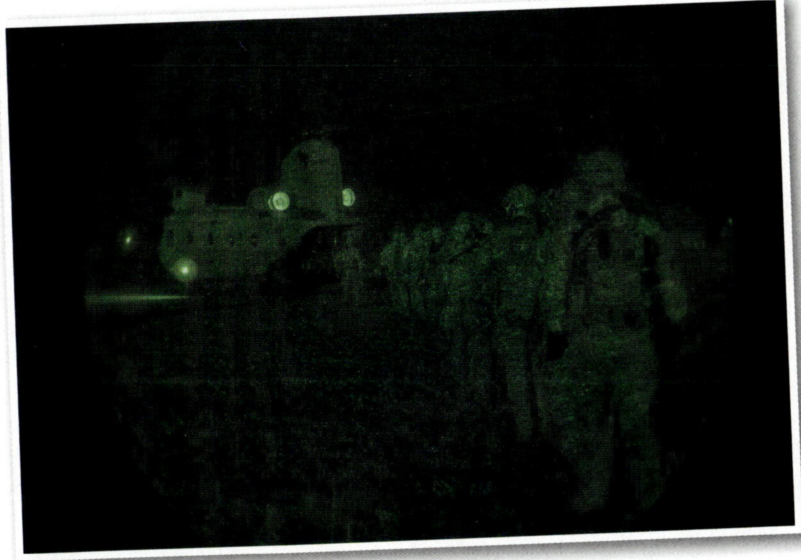

headquarters, the MI and Special Troops battalions and 3rd Ranger battalion are all stationed at Fort Moore, Georgia, while the 1st Ranger Battalion is at Hunter Army Airfield, at Fort Stewart, Georgia. The 2nd Ranger Battalion is at Joint Base Lewis-McChord, Washington.

All Rangers are airborne qualified so that the entire regiment can conduct parachute jumps as needed. They also frequently conduct air assault missions using helicopters. The regiment uses a variety of vehicles for mobility on the ground, including Humvees, light tactical trucks, and MRAPs. They were seen in Syria using Stryker infantry carriers, although those may have been borrowed for that specific mission.

The Rangers have one vehicle unique to their regiment, the Ranger Special Operations Vehicle (RSOV). This is based on the Land Rover Defender 110 series and is similar to vehicles used by the UK's SAS. The RSOV can be fitted with a variety of weapons including the M2 .50-calibre machine gun, Mk.19 40mm grenade launcher and smaller machine guns such as the M240 and M249. There is a medical variant for evacuating casualties and a mortar variant which can tow a 120mm mortar.

A soldier wishing to become a Ranger must volunteer and then pass the Ranger Selection and Assessment Program (RASP). This course teaches light infantry skills and evaluates the volunteer's suitability to be a member of the regiment. It is a very difficult course with failure rates typically over 50%. Students get little sleep or food during the eight-week course to build their ability to think and act under stress. Many graduates say passing the course is less dependent on learning all the training tasks and more about demonstrating willpower and determination.

Passing the course earns the new Ranger the coveted tan beret and Ranger tab for their uniform. Not all graduates go on to the regiment, however. Soldiers from across the army volunteer for Ranger School to test themselves and learn the skills taught there. They earn the tab but do not wear the beret unless in the regiment. Infantry NCOs and officers practically need the Ranger tab to move forward in their careers.

For those who join the regiment, they are now part of a small group who train constantly when not on operations, which are frequent. They are held to the highest standards of skills and behaviour and can be removed from the regiment if they don't measure up.

LEFT: A file of Rangers board a CH47 Chinook for a night air assault mission. Rangers are expert at nighttime infiltrations and assaults. (US ARMY)

BELOW: When Rangers are not on operations, they are training, such as this forcible entry exercise at Fort Moore. (US ARMY)

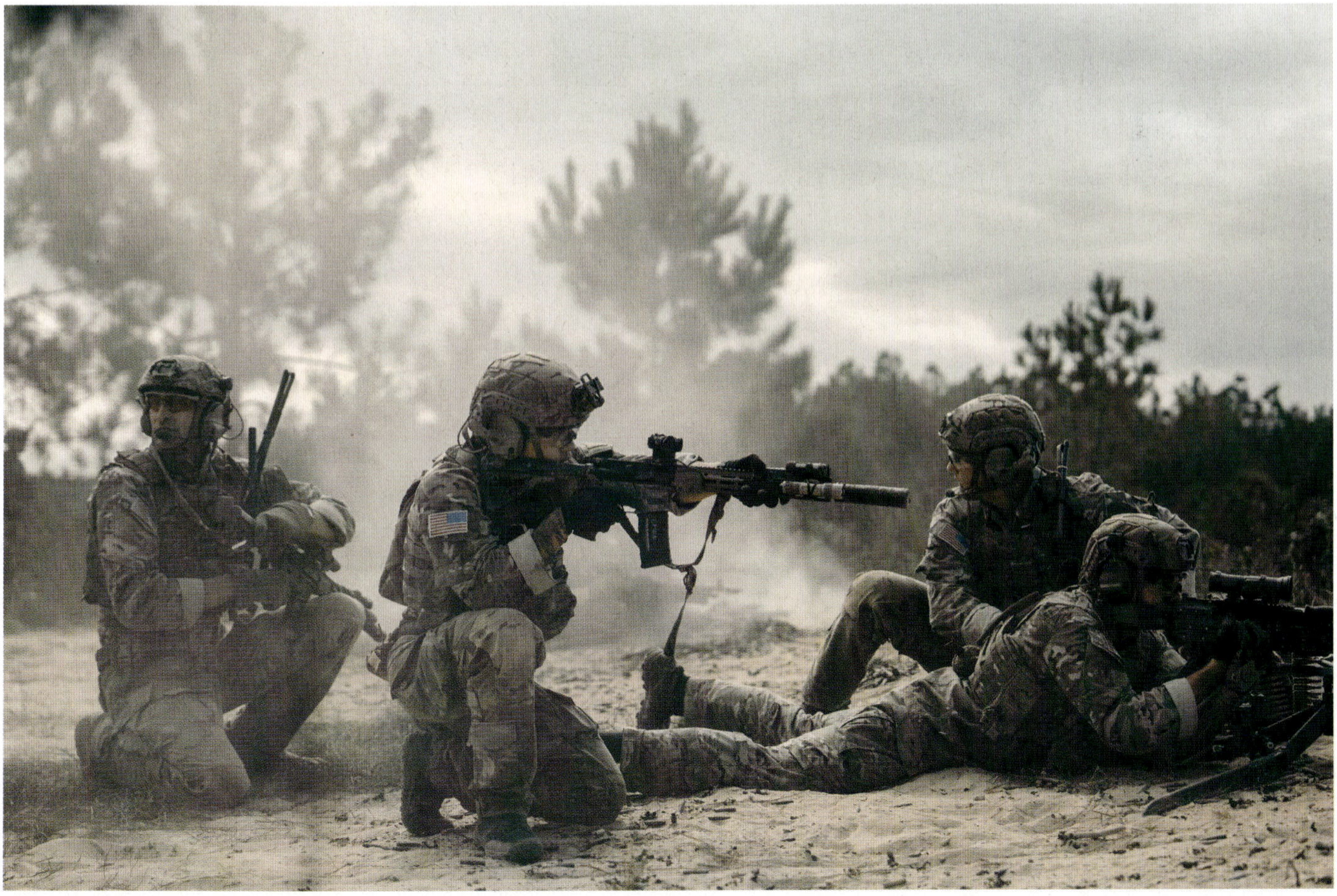

SUBSCRIBE TODAY
AND SAVE £££!

SUBSCRIBER BENEFITS

- **EXCLUSIVE** Subscriber offers on the Key Publishing Shop
- **SAVE** over buying individual issues
- **DELIVERED DIRECT** to your door
- **SUBSCRIBER DISCOUNTS** on Key Publishing event tickets
- **BE THE FIRST** to read the latest features

OUR LATEST SUBSCRIPTION OFFER

BEST VALUE

UK PRINT
1 YEAR
£58.99
Paying by Annual Direct Debit
GET TWO ISSUES FREE!

UK PRINT
1 YEAR
£64.99
Paying by Credit or Debit Card
GET ONE ISSUE FREE!

Please quote: CMV25 when ordering

SCAN THE QR CODE TO ORDER DIRECT FROM OUR SHOP

shop.keypublishing.com/cmvsubs

or call **+44 (0)1780 480404** (Lines open 9.00-5.30, Monday-Friday GMT)

Terms and conditions: Quoted rates are for UK subscriptions only, paying one year print or annual direct debit.
Standard one-year print subscription prices: UK - £64.99, EU - £71.99, USA - £83.99, ROW - £89.99.
All quoted prices subject to change. **CLOSING DATE: See website for full details.**

KEVIN WHEATCROFT TALKS FURY AND TIGER TANKS
www.keymilitary.com
CLASSIC
MILITARY
VEHICLE
KEY Publishing
£5.90
March 2025
ISSUE 286
03
9 771473 777218
UNMATCHED UTILITY
Model Build
1/35 scale
LRDG F30
Truck
Rare 1944 Buick
M39 Armoured
Utility Vehicle

Rebuilding a Renault
'Filmstar' R2087 workhorse restored

BRIXMIS on Tour
Cold War spy cars behind the Iron Curtain

SUBSCRIBE TODAY AND GET TWO ISSUES FREE!
300/25

National Guard

RIGHT: Two Pennsylvania Guardsmen compete in a Best Warrior competition. Their desert-pattern uniforms are actually chemical warfare suits. (US ARMY)

Of all the US Military's reserve components, the Army National Guard (ARNG) is the largest and most widely used. Its strength of 325,000 soldiers makes it larger than many nation's entire militaries. Along with the Army Reserve, it reinforces the Regular Army in time of war and, increasingly, for other military operations which include combat but are not formally declared wars. There are unique facets to the Guard which bear examination and clarification, particularly for non-American readers.

The Guard had its origins in the colonial militia system, which predated American independence. The militia was organised by the individual colonies (later states) and called up for service during emergencies. In the late 1800s the various state militias were organised into the National Guard, controlled by their parent states unless mobilised for federal service. In return, states received federal funding for their National Guard units.

Due to this heritage, the oldest units in the US Army are National Guard units, some of which trace their heritage to militia units which predate the Regular Army's creation by a century or more. As a result, older Guard units will have a numerical designation assigned by the Army when it reorganised prior to World War One. They will also have a link to a unit which existed prior to that time and may bear mottos and names from that older unit.

For example, the 181st Infantry Regiment of the Massachusetts National Guard is considered the oldest combat arms regiment in the army. Its heritage goes back to the North Regiment of militia, established

BELOW: A sergeant of a Tennessee Guard artillery unit learns how to use a Bulgarian Army BM-21 multiple rocket launcher during Exercise Thracian Warrior 24. (US ARMY)

in 1636. Technically, militia units from the colonial period began their service as part of the British Army! Most units were raised in the 1800s for the War of 1812 or American Civil War.

The title National Guard comes from the French National Guard (*Garde Nationale*) reserve force, adopted due to appreciation of French support during the American Revolution. Some New York militia units began to use the title in the early 1800s, and it was codified by the US Congress in the Militia Act of 1903.

This means each state has its own, independent military ground force, named for that state, for example, the Colorado Army National Guard. There is also an Air National Guard, which is a state-run reserve component of the US Air Force, so the term Army National Guard is used when needed for clarification. Each state's National Guard forces are under control of that state's elected governor, who can call it to service for emergencies such as civil disorder or natural disasters. Federal troops can be deployed for such internal events, but there are legal restrictions on their employment. Since Guard units are spread throughout a state, they are usually able to respond more quickly.

Each state has a military staff to oversee its units, led by a general officer known as The Adjutant General (TAG). The TAG is appointed by the »

ABOVE: An Abrams tanks of the Tennessee National Guard's 278th Armored Cavalry Regiment moves at Fort Cavazos, Texas during a brigade-level combat certification test. (US ARMY)

RIGHT: An Alaska National Guard UH60 uses a 'Bambi Bucket' to drop water during firefighting training. The bucket holds 630 gallons of water and can be refilled from nearby lakes or rivers. (US ARMY)

BELOW: A UH60 helicopter crew of the Idaho National Guard rescues an injured hiker in the Rocky Mountains. Some civil support missions, such as casualty evacuation, resemble military tasks. (US ARMY)

governor, who generally picks capable and qualified officers from within the state. The state headquarters is called Joint Forces Headquarters (JFHQ) as it oversees ground and air forces. Other US military units could be placed under a state's command if circumstances warrant.

National Guard recruits attend the same training schools as Regular Army soldiers and return home after graduating to join their unit. They serve a minimum of one weekend a month and a two-week annual training period. It is common for Guard members to serve more than this minimal requirement. Some members transfer in from other military branches, including the US Air Force, Navy, and Marine Corps. The Guard's size and distribution throughout a state's communities often makes it easier to continue military service there.

Decades ago, the National Guard rarely deployed out of its state and was underfunded and often equipped with obsolete weapons and kit. However, since the late 1990s, the Guard has been deployed more frequently and consequently funding, training and equipment have been vastly improved. While sometimes chided as 'weekend warriors,' anyone who joins the Guard now knows they will likely be deployed overseas at least once during their six to eight-year term of service and there is a good chance they will serve in a combat zone.

As the National Guard has a domestic mission within its state, it is also probable a Guard soldier will see service within the United States. Referred to as a 'State Activation,' it is usually for local problems such as wildfires, blizzards, floods, and hurricanes. During these situations Guard units provide lifesaving help such as evacuation and medical assistance. They also help in recovery efforts such as clearing roads, distributing clean water and food, and search and rescue.

They can also be activated for civil disturbances such as riots. While Guard units are equipped and capable of riot control missions, Americans have a tradition of not using military forces against civilians. Therefore, using Guard troops for such duties is held as a last resort if the local police are unable to restore order.

Though it has its share of support units, virtually all of the US Army's reserve combat arms units are in the National Guard. This includes eight infantry divisions, some of which have armoured units in their table of organisation. Other combat forces include eight field artillery brigades, three air defence artillery brigades and two special forces groups.

Much of the army's artillery strength is in the National Guard, including numerous HIMARS battalions.

As the HIMARS rocket/missile launcher has proven very effective and is in high demand, these units deploy often for training, exercises, and combat missions. Experience has shown the field artillery general support mission is well within Guard readiness capabilities, and its artillery brigades would be very effective as corps and field army assets.

The dual military and civil missions of the National Guard can be difficult at times. Guard units have limited training time available but must be ready for both their wartime mission and for state service, which is generally of a noncombat nature and require different mindsets and task details. The Regular Army wants Guard units ready to go into combat, performing their wartime tasks. A state's governor, however, wants an artillery unit to use its ammunition trucks to carry emergency supplies, an aviation battalion to use its helicopters for search and rescue and firefighting, and an engineer company to clear debris and repair roads washed out by floods. Guard units must always balance these competing responsibilities.

The 100th Missile Defense Brigade is a unique Guard unit based in Colorado. It oversees missile defence for the United States using a system of radars and satellite networks to detect and track threatening missile launches. It can launch ground-based interceptor missiles against an incoming attack. Though part of the National Guard, this unit is always on duty and has subordinate units in California, Alaska, and New York, including some Regular Army soldiers. Soldiers typically stay in this unit for long periods to develop the required technical skills. The unit is part of the US Army's Space and Missile Defense Command (SMDC).

Guard units see frequent deployments worldwide. This includes missions to the Middle East as part of task forces which act as deterrent forces against any widening of the current conflicts in Syria and Israel. Though not widely reported, US troops, including Guardsmen, take part in combat operations when needed. National Guard units also take part in exercises in Europe as part of NATO and in the Pacific Region with various partner nations.

The US Army recognises the large role played by National Guard forces and is increasingly incorporating them in army transformation efforts. South Carolina Guardsmen recently field tested the new XM7 rifle (see page 91), while Tennessee Guard artillerymen used the Autonomous Multi-domain Launcher to fire Precision Strike Missiles at a decommissioned ship during exercise Valiant Strike 24 (see page 28). Guard soldiers are also testing and experimenting with new UAS.

While this is a tacit admission that the US Army is not large enough to meet its commitments without extensive use of the reserve components, there are advantages. Guard units are now better equipped and trained than in the past. Their soldiers have more operational experience and joint service with other US military branches and foreign forces as well. This means that in the event of a major war, the National Guard is able to quickly commit major combat forces.

LEFT: The National Guard provides much of the army's strength for Middle East operations. This officer of the Colorado National Guard's 169th Field Artillery Brigade has deployed there twice with this unit, most recently as its commander. (US ARMY)

LEFT: One of the most common images American citizens have of National Guard soldiers is seeing them carrying food and water supplies after a natural disaster. (US ARMY)

BELOW: Two Texas National Guard M142 HIMARS rocket launchers fire during an exercise at Grafenwoehr, Germany. This Texas unit was on a rotational deployment to Europe. (US ARMY)

Army Reserve

Vital support to the total force

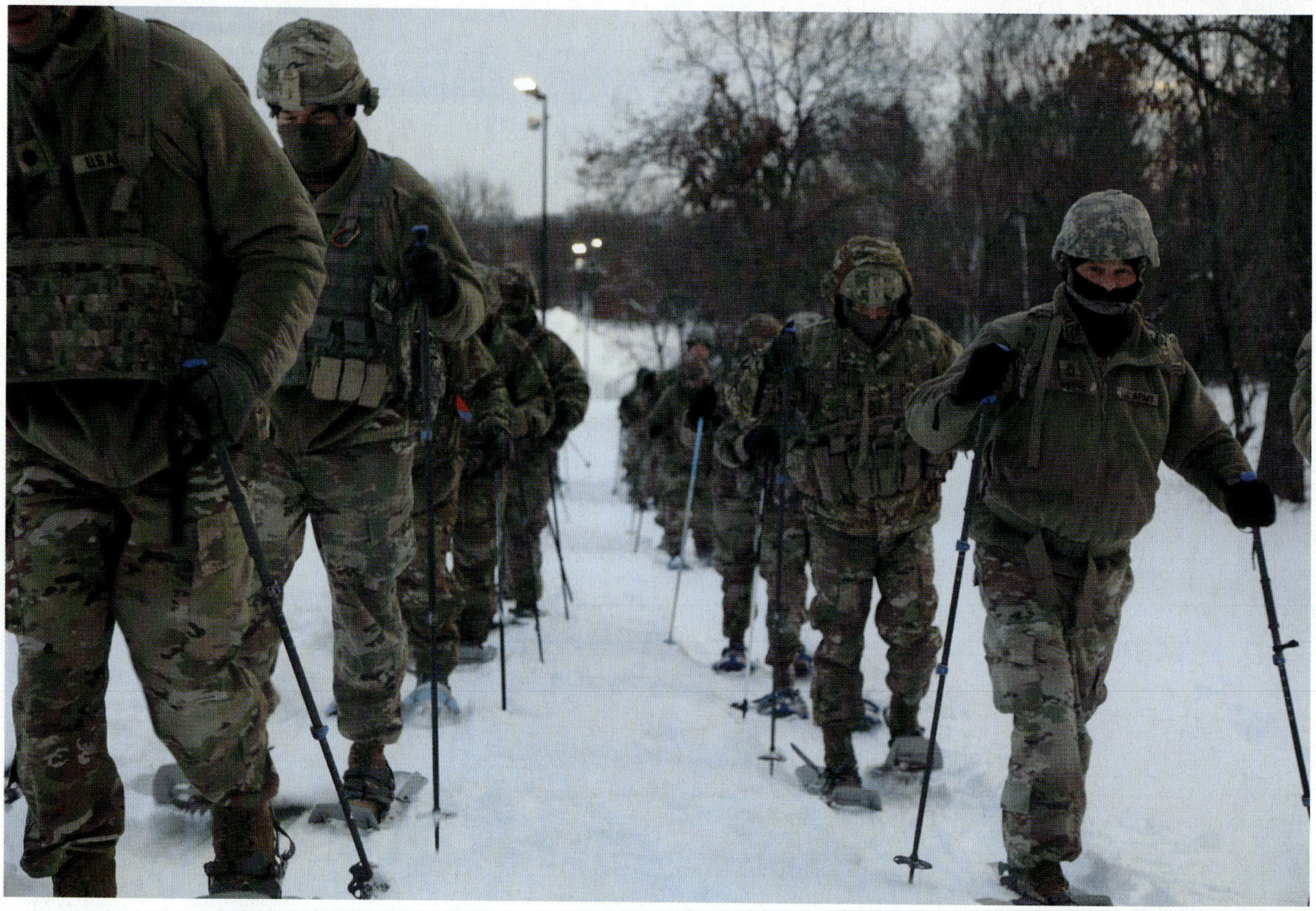

ABOVE: Reservists of the 88th Training Division during snowshoe training at Fort McCoy, Wisconsin. (US ARMY)

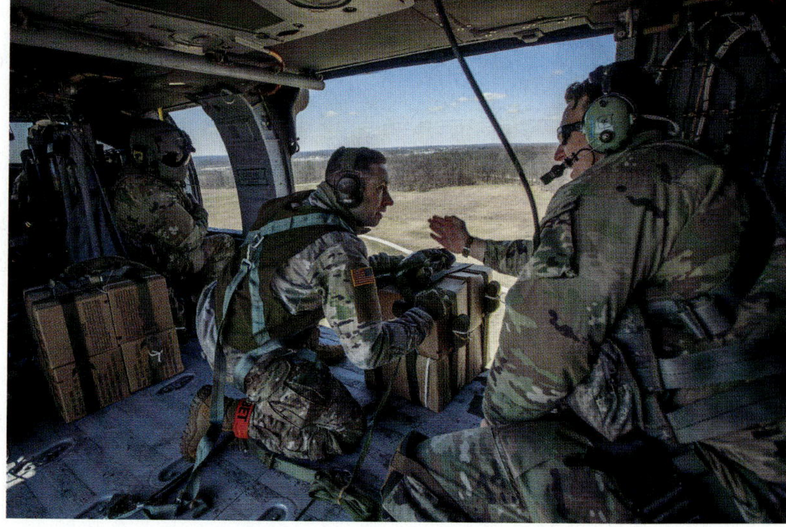

The US Army Reserve is the federally organised and operated reserve force of the total US Army, which also includes the Regular Army and Army National Guard. Like the National Guard, citizens can enlist directly into the Army Reserve, spend their entire military career there and retire from it after 20 years of service. Unlike the National Guard, the Reserve is always under the control of the federal government.

There are three kinds of reservist. The Selected Reserve perform what is generally thought of as reserve service. After their initial training, which is conducted alongside Regular and Guard troops, they return home and join a local reserve unit. They typically train one weekend a month along with a two-week annual training (AT) event. Most Selected Reservists fall into this category, but there are also Individual Mobilization Augmentees (IMA). These are soldiers who do not train with a unit as described above but are attached to a headquarters with whom they would serve if mobilised. Most IMAs train with that unit for two weeks or more per year.

The Individual Ready Reserve (IRR) contains soldiers who can be called up as individuals if needed to fill vacancies in Regular, Guard, or Reserve units. US Citizens who

RIGHT: Reserve soldiers from aviation, quartermaster, and civil affairs units practice air dropping supplies by helicopter at Camp Atterbury, Indiana. (US ARMY)

join any branch of the US military have an eight-year service obligation. In the army, soldiers who serve on active duty or in the Guard or Selected Reserve for less than eight years are automatically placed in the IRR for the remainder of their obligation. For example, a soldier who serves in the Regular Army for four years will be placed in the IRR for four years unless they opt to enter the Guard or Selected Reserve. IRR soldiers are considered inactive and do not train unless they volunteer to do so.

The Retired Reserve consists of soldiers who have retired from any component of the US Army after 20 or more years of service. They are liable for recall to service in an emergency, though this rarely occurs. More often retirees volunteer to return to duty to fill critical vacancies. All told there are about 350,000 soldiers in the Army Reserve, with 190,000 in the Selected Reserve. One little known fact is that most officer's commissions in the US Army are reserve commissions, as only a small number of 'Regular' commissions are available.

The Selected Reserve provides complete units that can be mobilised for active service, and they frequently train with active units. There is only one combat arms unit in the Army Reserve, the 100th Infantry Battalion, 442nd Infantry Regiment, in honour of the Japanese American soldiers who served in World War Two. All other combat arms units are in the National Guard. The rest of the reserve's units are combat support units which are vital to keeping an army in the field. Certain types of units exist primarily in the Army Reserve (see table). For example, 86% of the army's civil affairs units are in the reserve. This makes sense, as reservists spend most of their time in the civilian world and are naturally more able to relate to civil issues. Reserve units have technical and logistical skills which are more

compatible with occupations in civil society.

In addition to complete support units, the Army Reserve contains three training commands with ten training divisions across the nation. These are not full-strength divisions; rather, these units are maintained as training cadres with several major roles. In the event of a major war, these units would train the tens of thousands of volunteers or conscripts called to service. They would also give refresher training to soldiers recalled from the IRR or Retired Reserve. During peacetime, they run schools which soldiers can attend to learn new skills and prepare for future promotion. There are also Mission Support Commands and Readiness Divisions. These provide support to other army units within an assigned region.

In wartime, the troops trained by these units would be used as replacements for casualties in existing units or formed into new units. New units manned by conscripts are known as the Army of the United States (AUS). They are called to service by the US Congress. This term was first used in 1940 when the army expanded for World War Two but has not been used since the 1970s. It could be used again in the event of a major war.

As the army transforms for future battlefields, the Army Reserve transforms as well. A few reserve units are testing new equipment and tactics, as it is important to see how well reserve soldiers and units can adapt and use these tools. The Ukraine War has shown how many new tools, such as UAS, are distributed across the force and used at all levels and by combat and support units alike. If the United States goes to war, these part time soldiers will quickly find themselves on full-time battlefields.

LEFT: Soldiers from reserve civil affairs and psychological operations units train with special forces troops at Camp Shelby, Mississippi. These types of units frequently work with special forces so they must keep up their basic combat skills. (US ARMY)

BELOW: These reservists of the 43rd Multi-Role Bridge Company are constructing a 'Wet Gap' crossing for combat units during the DEFENDER 24 exercise in Poland. (US ARMY)

Percentages of selected unit types within the US Army Reserve	
Unit Type	**Percentage**
Civil Affairs	86%
Psychological Operations	83%
Quartermaster	59%
Medical	55%
Transportation	44%
Public Affairs	38%
Engineer	35%
Military Police	25%
Space Operations	24%

Fire Teams to Field Armies

Combat organisation

As the US Army prepares for future warfare, it has returned to the division as the basic fighting unit for conflict with a peer/near-peer opponent. The brigade combat team (BCT) still exists as a functional component of the division. During the wars in Iraq and Afghanistan, brigades were flexible and with suitable attachments could operate effectively in a counterinsurgency role under a regional command. However, for high intensity warfare a BCT is not big enough: divisions bring needed capability to that kind of fight.

For a modern war the army is looking forward while taking a few pages from its history books. The Cold War US Army was well organised to take on the Soviet Union. Some of those concepts are appropriate for the current situation. This is why the army is going back to the division and why divisions regained the Divisional Artillery (DIVARTY) in their makeup. The return of DIVARTY is a work in progress and not all divisions have them. Simultaneously, the army is examining new types of units, such as the Multi-Functional Reconnaissance Company, and how best to employ new technologies. For example, many Ukrainian units have a dedicated unit of UAS operators. The US Army is experimenting to see how such units might fit within battalions and BCTs.

Whatever the technologies, army units are still organised along traditional lines and their true effectiveness comes from their soldiers. A soldier's unit is their home and their squad (sometimes called a section or team, depending on the type of unit) and platoon is their family. The company and battalion are the next echelon - a soldier knows some people within them and is proud of their affiliation. Any echelon beyond the battalion is more abstract - the soldier knows about them but rarely interacts with them. Soldiers fight for each other, and instilling esprit de corps in the squad, platoon, and company are vital for unit cohesion.

Team: This is the basic building block of the army. Called a fire team in the infantry, it contains four soldiers: an automatic rifleman with an M249 Squad Automatic Weapon, a grenadier whose rifle has a 40mm grenade launcher attached to it, and two riflemen, one of whom is the team leader, a junior non-commissioned officer.

Squad: Comprised of two teams led by a sergeant or staff sergeant, the squad is the backbone of an infantry unit. One team can manoeuvre while the other acts as a base-of-fire element, providing covering fire for the moving team.

Platoon: Platoons generally consist of three or four squads. In an infantry platoon one squad might be a weapons squad armed with M240 machine guns and Javelin missiles. Platoons are commanded by a lieutenant, called the platoon leader, with a staff sergeant or sergeant first class as platoon sergeant.

Company: These are the smallest units which are able to function on their own on the battlefield, though only for limited time without support. They are commanded by a captain, with a first lieutenant as executive officer (XO) and a first sergeant as the senior NCO. Infantry companies usually have a weapons platoon with mortars and machine guns. In the field artillery, company sized units are called batteries and they have from four to eight cannon or rocket launchers, depending on type. In cavalry and armour units, they are called troops.

LEFT: A 2nd lieutenant leads his tank platoon to the firing line for a live fire exercise in South Korea. (US ARMY)

Battalion: Battalions have four to six companies: infantry battalions normally have three rifle companies, a weapons company, a support company and a headquarters company. They can also conduct limited independent operations. Armour and cavalry units of this size are called squadrons. They are commanded by a lieutenant colonel, with a major as XO and a command sergeant major as senior enlisted advisor to the commander.

Brigade: Also known as a Brigade Combat Team (BCT), this echelon has three or more battalions. A few brigade sized units are called regiments but are organised similarly. A typical BCT has three manoeuvre battalions (infantry, armour or combined arms), and a battalion each of engineers and support troops. Some BCTs retain an artillery battalion as well. BCTs are commanded by a colonel, with a lieutenant colonel as XO and a command sergeant major as enlisted advisor.

Division: These are the basic fighting units of the army. They are commanded by a major general with two deputy commanders, one for manoeuvre and one for support. Each is a brigadier general, and the division also has a command sergeant major. Divisions have two to four BCTs, along with a DIVARTY, aviation brigade, sustainment brigade and headquarters battalion.

Corps: A corps comprises two to five divisions with additional support assets such as extra battalions or brigades of artillery, engineers and aviation. They are commanded by a lieutenant general. Corps are the highest echelon that provide directions and orders for combat operations.

Field Army: A general commands a field army, which contains two or more corps with appropriate support units. Currently, the numbered field armies also have a geographic area of responsibility (see table).

US Army Field Army Designations	
Field Army	**Commands army forces for:**
First Army	Serves as a mobilisation, readiness and training command
Third Army	US Central Command (Middle East)
Fifth Army	US Northern Command (North America)
Sixth Army	US Southern Command (Central and South America)
Seventh Army	US European Command
Eighth Army	US Army Forces Korea
Ninth Army	US Africa Command

BELOW: A fire team of paratroopers from the 173rd Airborne Brigade attack an objective during a training mission in Germany. (US ARMY)

1st Cavalry Division

One of the US Army's most famous combat divisions, the 'First Cav' is also the one which has changed the most over its history. The army activated the unit on September 13, 1921, organised as a horse cavalry division. It remained so during the 1920s and 30s, though there were experiments with mechanisation as World War Two began.

By 1943 the army recognised the obsolescence of horse cavalry and while the division retained the

1st Cavalry Division
1st Armored Brigade Combat Team 'Ironhorse'
2nd BN, 5th Cavalry Regiment 'Lancers'
2nd BN 8th Cavalry Regiment 'Stallions'
2nd BN, 12th Cavalry Regiment 'Thunder Horse'
2nd Armored Brigade Combat Team 'Black Jack'
1st BN, 5th Cavalry Regiment 'Black Knights'
1st BN, 8th Cavalry Regiment 'Mustangs'
1st BN 9th Cavalry Regiment 'Headhunters'
3rd Armored Brigade Combat Team 'Greywolf'
2nd BN 7th Cavalry Regiment 'Ghost'
3rd BN, 8th Cavalry Regiment 'Warhorse'
1st BN, 12th Cavalry Regiment 'Chargers'
Division Artillery 'Red Team'
3rd BN, 16th Field Artillery Regiment 'Rolling Thunder'
1st BN, 82nd Field Artillery Regiment 'Dragons'
2nd BN, 82nd Field Artillery Regiment 'Steel Dragons'
6th BN, 56th Air Defense Artillery 'Nighthawks'

The division also has a HQ BN, Aviation BDE and Sustainment BDE	Each BCT has a HQ element, recce element, engineer BN and a support BN

cavalry designation, it converted to an infantry formation. The division deployed to Australia and was soon embroiled in the Pacific War, entering combat in the Admiralty Islands in February 1944. It then fought in the Philippines and went into occupation duty in Japan when the war ended.

When the Korean War began in 1950 the 1st Cavalry Division was rushed to the Korean Peninsula, where it fought until 1952 before returning to Japan. In 1957 the division returned to Korea, remaining there until 1965. Back in the United States, the army created a new type of division which used helicopters, then a still-new invention, to quickly move around the battlefield. The 11th Airborne Division served as the test unit for this concept, but when activated,

the army redesignated the division as the 1st Air Cavalry Division, while the unit in Korea became the 2nd Infantry Division.

This new heliborne unit achieved fame in the Vietnam war. It proved the concept of what is now called air assault operations. After Vietnam the 1st Cavalry Division converted into an armoured division, which it remains today. In this form the unit saw action in the Gulf War, Balkans, and Iraq. Some elements served in Afghanistan and against the so-called Islamic State.

The division is based at Fort Cavazos, Texas. It is part of the US III Armored Corps. The division has made frequent contributions to US forces in Europe during the current Ukraine War crisis.

1st Armored Division

America's tank division

Stationed at Fort Bliss, Texas, the 1st Armored Division, historically known as 'Old Ironsides', has more recently taken on the moniker 'America's Tank Division', as it is the only armored division currently in active service. As a heavy division, it brings extensive firepower to the battlefield, able to smash through enemy formations through a combination of tanks, infantry fighting vehicles, artillery, and attack helicopters. It reports to the III Armored Corps as its higher headquarters.

The army activated the division on July 15, 1940, as it prepared for World War Two. As the first tank division in the army, it pioneered many of the training, doctrine, and tank gunnery procedures for US armoured forces. The 1st Armored Division entered the war in November 1942 during the landings in French North Africa, Operation Torch. After the Germans surrendered in North Africa the division took part in the invasion of Sicily. Next, 1st Armored went to mainland Italy, ending the war in the Po Valley in May 1945.

Deactivated after the war, the division was returned to service during the American military buildup for the Korean War. It remained at Fort Hood, Texas, until 1971 when the division transferred to Germany as part of the US contribution to NATO. After the Cold War it took part in the 1991 Gulf War, operations in Kosovo, and the wars in Iraq, Afghanistan, and against the so-called Islamic State.

Currently the division is posted at Fort Bliss, Texas and takes part in exercises and support operations

1st Armored Division
1st Armored Brigade Combat Team 'Ready First'
1st BN, 36th Infantry Regiment 'Spartans'
2nd BN 37th Armored Regiment 'Iron Dukes'
4th BN, 70th Armored Regiment 'Thunderbolts'
2nd Armored Brigade Combat Team 'Iron Brigade'
1st BN, 6th Infantry Regiment 'Regulars'
1st BN, 35th Armored Regiment 'Conquerors'
1st BN, 37th Armored Regiment 'Bandits'
Armored Brigade Combat Team 'Bulldog'
4th BN, 6th Infantry Regiment 'Regulars'
1st BN, 67th Armored Regiment 'Death Dealers'
1st BN, 77th Armored Regiment 'Steel Tiger'
Division Artillery 'Iron Steel'
4th BN, 1st Field Artillery Regiment
2nd BN, 3rd Field Artillery Regiment 'Gunners'
4th BN, 27th Field Artillery Regiment 'Iron Thunder'
4th BN, 60th Air Defense Artillery Regiment

The division also has a HQ BN, Aviation BDE and Sustainment BDE

Each BCT has a HQ element, recce element, engineer BN and a support BN

worldwide, including Europe, Africa, South America, Asia, and the Indo-Pacific. As of this writing, it is active in 20 countries, show the value of armoured forces even in regions thought inhospitable to tanks. As a heavy division, its brigades are frequently sent to Europe to take part in ongoing support to NATO due to the Ukraine War.

LEFT: A tank from 4th Battalion, 70th Armored Regiment, moves down a trail during gunnery qualifications in South Korea during a 2024 deployment to support US /South Korean training. (US ARMY)

LEFT: An M1A2 Abrams fires a round during the 1st Armored Division's best tank crew competition in 2024. The winners went on to compete in an army-wide contest. (US ARMY)

1st Infantry Division

ABOVE: A soldier of the 1st Battalion, 16th Infantry Regiment carries ammunition for his Bradley IFV during gunnery training. (US ARMY)

RIGHT: The army uses hand to hand combat training to encourage martial spirit and confidence. These 1st Infantry Division soldiers are taking part in a divisional tournament. (US ARMY)

The 1st Infantry Division, created on May 24, 1917, is the oldest division in the US Army, having never been deactivated since its creation. It is also one of the better-known divisions, partly due to its exploits and partly to its distinctive shoulder patch of a large red number one on a green background.

The unit saw extensive combat in World War One, taking part in several operations, suffering over 23,000 casualties. Notably, the division had a mascot, a stray dog named Rags. His acute hearing allowed him to hear incoming artillery fire before the soldiers could. The troops quickly learned that when Rags took cover, they should do the same.

During World War Two the division landed in North Africa and took part in the invasion of Sicily. It returned to England to train for the invasion of Europe. The division gained fame for the fighting on Omaha Beach on D-Day. It also fought at Aachen, the Hurtgen Forest and the Battle of the Bulge. Seventeen soldiers from the division were awarded the Medal of Honor during the war.

During the Korean War, the 1st Infantry Division went to Germany as a deterrent against Soviet invasion. It returned to the US in 1955, stationed at Fort Riley, Kansas, which has remained its home station ever since. The division saw extensive service in Vietnam, the Gulf War, the Balkans, and all the operations in Middle East.

Since 2017, the 1st Infantry Division has made numerous deployments to Europe under Operation Atlantic Resolve, a programme designed to reinforce NATO due to Russia's invasion of the Donbass and subsequent invasion of Ukraine. Though an infantry division, it is currently organised more as an armoured unit.

In June 2024, a detachment went to the UK to take part in the commemoration of the 80th Anniversary of the Normandy landings. In 1944 the division occupied the military keep in Dorchester and so participated in the ceremonies there.

1st Infantry Division
1st Armored Brigade Combat Team 'Devil Brigade'
1st BN, 16th Infantry Regiment 'Iron Rangers'
2nd BN, 34 Armored Regiment 'Dreadnaughts'
3rd BN, 66th Armored Regiment 'Burt's Knights'
2nd Armored Brigade Combat Team 'Dagger Brigade'
1st BN, 18th Infantry Regiment 'Vanguards'
1st BN 63rd Armored Regiment 'Dragons'
2nd BN, 70th Armored Regiment 'Thunderbolts'
Division Artillery
1st BN, 5th Field Artillery Regiment 'Hamilton's Own'
1st BN, 7th Field Artillery Regiment 'First Lightning'

The division also has a HQ BN, Aviation BDE and Sustainment BDE	Each BCT has a HQ element, recce element, engineer BN and a support BN

2nd Infantry Division

The 2nd Infantry Division, headquartered at Camp Humphreys, South Korea, occupies several unique roles in the US Army's divisional structure. It is the only permanently forward stationed division in the army, being based in South Korea. All other divisions are based in United States territory. It is also the only US Army division to be combined with the army of another nation. The South Korean (Republic of Korea - ROK) Army contributes forces to the division on a rotational basis.

The 2nd Infantry Division arrived in Korea after a distinguished history in both World Wars. The US Army created the division on September 21, 1917, as it struggled to gather forces for the United State's entry into World War One. Due to personnel shortages, the unit deployed to Europe with a brigade of US Marines. The division fought well in several battles and campaigns. During World War Two the division went ashore at Omaha Beach on June 7, 1944, the day after the initial landings. It fought extensively in the Normandy campaign and subsequently saw action in the Ardennes and Germany.

The unit was among the first American units deployed for the Korean War in 1950. After the war it returned to the US but in 1965 went back to Korea due to a shuffling of units when the 1st Cavalry Division became an airmobile unit. It has remained in Korea ever since, with some units deploying to Iraq and Afghanistan.

Currently the division acts mainly as a headquarters for rotating units from other divisions and the rotating ROK mechanised brigade. The US Army typically rotates armoured or Stryker brigades. In wartime the division would likely employ BCTs quickly deployed from the United States and coordinate with the capable ROK army.

LEFT: A soldier of the 2nd Infantry Division carries a simulated casualty to safety during a combined exercise. (US ARMY)

2nd Infantry Division	
1 Rotational BCT from the United States	
Currently, the 1st Stryker Brigade Combat Team of the 7th Infantry Division	
1 Rotational Brigade from ROK Army	
Division Artillery	
210th Field Artillery Brigade 'Thunder'	
6th BN, 37th Field Artillery Regiment	
1st BN, 38th Field Artillery Regiment	
1 Rotational BN	
The division also has a HQ BN, Aviation BDE and Sustainment BDE	The artillery BNs are equipped with M270A1 MLRS

LEFT: South Korean and American soldiers train together regularly. Here they are acting as a security element on a rooftop. (US ARMY)

3rd Infantry Division

RIGHT: Soldiers of the 3rd Infantry Division's 2nd Armored BCT pose with the speaker of the Lithuanian Parliament during a deployment in January 2024. (US ARMY)

BELOW RIGHT: An M1A2 tank prepares to assault through a breached obstacle during the Marne Focus exercise, where the division's soldiers validate their skills and training. (US ARMY)

Stationed at Fort Stewart, Georgia, the 3rd Infantry Division is attached to the XVIII Airborne Corps, providing the heavy armoured punch for the US Army's rapid response forces. Similar to the 1st Infantry Division, the 3rd is organised as an armoured division, currently with two Armoured BCTs.

As of writing, the division's two artillery battalions are still assigned to the BCTs rather than centralised in the Divisional Artillery. The DIVARTY headquarters element has training oversight of both battalions even though they remain under the BCT's functional control. Further, the DIVARTY has four non-artillery battalions assigned to it, including a signals battalion, chemical battalion, engineer battalion, and intelligence and electronic warfare battalion. These units fall under the DIVARTY as part of army transformation efforts to create its future fighting force.

The division dates to World War One, created on November 21, 1917. The unit's nickname, 'Rock of the Marne', from its steadfastness during the Second Battle of the Marne in July 1918. During a German attack, other Allied units retreated, but the 3rd Division remained in place and held their position against determined German attacks. During World War Two the unit was the only US division to fight on all fronts in Europe, including North Africa, Sicily, Italy, France, and Germany. It fought in Korea but spent the rest of the Cold War in West Germany. The 3rd also saw combat in the Gulf War, Iraq, and Afghanistan.

The most famous member of the division is the classic action film actor of the late 1940s, 50s and 60s, Audie Murphy, the most decorated US soldier of World War Two. He earned every award for valour available in the US Army, including the Medal of Honor.

3rd Infantry Division
1st Armored Brigade Combat Team 'Raider'
2nd BN, 7th Infantry Regiment 'Cottonbalers'
3rd BN, 69th Infantry Regiment 'Speed and Power'
1st BN, 64th Armored Regiment 'Desert Rogue'
1st BN, 41st Field Artillery Regiment 'Glory's Guns'
2nd Armored Brigade Combat Team :Spartans'
3rd BN, 15th Infantry Regiment 'Old China Hands'
3rd BN 67th Armored Regiment 'Hounds of Hell'
2nd BN 69th Armored Regiment 'Panthers'
1st BN, 9th Field Artillery Regiment 'Battlekings'
Divisional Artillery 'Marne Thunder'
63rd Expeditionary Signal BN
83rd Chemical BN
92nd Engineer BN
103rd Intelligence and Electronic Warfare BN

The division also has a HQ BN, Aviation BDE and Sustainment BDE

Each BCT has a HQ element, recce element, engineer BN and a support BN

4th Infantry Division

The 4th Infantry Division ranks among the US Army's longest serving divisions. While not as famous as some other units, its record of service is impressive. It is currently stationed at Fort Carson, Colorado. The unit's nickname, the 'Ivy Division', is a play on the unit's number when shown in Roman numerals as IV.

The division is organised with three BCTs, two are Stryker brigades while the third is an armoured brigade. It is the only division in the US Army to have this mix of units. In July 2024, the cavalry reconnaissance squadrons in both Stryker BCTs were inactivated, as the army is moving away from heavily armed reconnaissance units in favour of UAS and new technologies. The armoured BCT retains its cavalry squadron as of writing.

The 4th also retains its artillery battalions within the BCTs rather than consolidating them under a DIVARTY organisation. The DIVARTY headquarters still oversees training for the artillery battalions while they remain under the control of their respective BCTs. The Stryker BCTS are equipped with M777 towed 155mm howitzers while the Armoured BCT uses the M109 Paladin.

The division's 2nd Stryker BCT recently did a rotational tour in South Korea, attached to the 2nd Infantry Division. Such rotations allow a wide number of US Army units and soldiers to have experience operating on the Korean Peninsula, useful in case of conflict.

Created on December 10, 1917, the division took part in two campaigns during World War One.

Its service in World War Two was extensive, including fighting in Normandy, the Hurtgen Forest and the Ardennes. It saw further service in Vietnam, Iraq, and Afghanistan. It currently makes regular contributions to the US rotational forces in Europe.

ABOVE: An AH64 Apache attack helicopter of the 4th Infantry Division does gunnery training with its 30mm cannon at Fort Carson Colorado. (US ARMY)

ABOVE: Troops of the division's 2nd Stryker BCT carry out a combined arms live fire exercise at night during a rotation to South Korea. The unit's ability to operate at night has been used extensively in recent conflicts. (US ARMY)

4th Infantry Division
1st Stryker Brigade Combat Team 'Raiders'
1st BN 38th Infantry Regiment 'Rock of the Marne'
4th BN, 9th Infantry Regiment 'Manchu'
2nd BN 23rd Infantry Regiment 'Tomahawk'
2nd Bn, 12th Field Artillery Regiment 'Viking'
2nd Stryker Brigade Combat Team 'Mountain Warrior'
1st Bn 12th Infantry Regiment 'Red Warriors'
2nd BN 12th Infantry Regiment 'Lethal Warriors'
1st Bn 41st Infantry Regiment 'Straight and Stalwart'
2nd BN 77th Field Artillery Regiment 'Steel'
3rd Armored Brigade Combat Team 'Iron'
1st BN 8th Infantry Regiment 'Fighting Eagles'
1st BN 66th Armored Regiment 'Iron Knights'
1st BN 68th Armored Regiment 'Silver Lions'
3rd Bn 29th Field Artillery Regiment 'Pacesetters'

The division also has a HQ BN, Artillery HQ, Aviation BDE and Sustainment BDE

Each BCT has a HQ element, engineer BN and a support BN. 3rd ABCT has a recce BN

7th Infantry Division

The Bayonet Division

ABOVE: Soldiers of the 5th Battalion, 20th Infantry Regiment form a firing line alongside their Stryker vehicle during training at Joint Base Lewis-McChord. (US ARMY)

RIGHT: 7th Infantry Division artillerymen and Thai artillerymen load an M198 155mm Howitzer during Exercise Cobra Gold in Thailand, March 2024. (US ARMY)

Also known as the Hourglass Division, the 7th Infantry Division was activated on December 6, 1917. It saw limited action in World War One and was reactivated in 1940. During World War Two it fought in the Aleutian and Marshall Islands, the Philippines and Okinawa. The division was on occupation duty in Japan when the Korean War began and was soon in action there. It stayed in Korea until 1971 before returning to the United States. Afterward it was reorganised as a light division and took part in the invasion of Panama in 1989. In 1994 the division was inactivated as part of the post-Cold War army reductions.

7th Infantry Division	
1st Stryker Brigade Combat Team 'Ghost'	
2nd BN, 3rd Infantry Regiment 'The Old Guard'	
5th BN, 20th Infantry Regiment 'Sykes Regulars'	
1st BN 23rd Infantry Regiment 'Tomahawks'	
1st BN, 37th Field Artillery Regiment 'Red Lions'	
2nd Stryker Brigade Combat Team 'Lancer'	
2nd BN, 1st Infantry Regiment 'Legion'	
1st BN 17th Infantry Regiment 'Buffaloes'	
4th BN 23rd Infantry Regiment 'Tomahawks'	
2nd BN 17th Field Artillery Regiment 'Steel'	
The division also has an Aviation BDE	Each BCT has a HQ element, recce element, engineer BN and a support BN

In 1999 the army reactivated the 7th Division as a training command for the National Guard but again deactivated it in 2006. The next reactivation came in 2012 at Joint Base Lewis-McChord, Washington, again as an administrative headquarters overseeing training and equipment for the units at that base. In August 2024 two Stryker Brigade Combat Teams were assigned to the division.

Currently the division's primary focus is on the Pacific region, along with the 25th Infantry and 11th Airborne Divisions. It is not a full-strength division, lacking a third brigade and a DIVARTY. In the event of war its two brigades could be used to bring the 11th and 25th to full strength or it could be reinforced to full strength using brigades and support units from the Regular Army or the reserve components.

Two significant milestones for the division occurred in 2023-2024. In September 2023 Major General Michelle Schmidt took command of the division. She is the first woman to command a combat division in the US Army. In late 2024 the Stryker brigades formally adopted the 7th Infantry Division shoulder patch, replacing the 2nd Division patch the two brigades wore previously.

10th Mountain Division

Climb to Glory

10th Mountain Division
1st Infantry Brigade Combat Team 'Warrior'
2nd BN, 22nd Infantry Regiment 'Triple Deuce'
1st BN, 32nd Infantry Regiment 'Chosin'
1st BN, 87th Infantry Regiment 'Summit'
3rd Bn 6th Field Artillery Regiment 'Centaur'
2nd Infantry Brigade Combat Team 'Commando'
2nd BN 14th Infantry Regiment 'Golden Dragons'
4th BN, 31st Infantry Regiment 'Polar Bears'
2nd BN, 87th Infantry Regiment 'Catamounts'
2nd BN 15th Field Artillery Regiment 'Fighting 15th'
3rd Infantry Brigade Combat Team 'Patriot'
2nd BN, 2nd Infantry Regiment 'Ramrods'
2nd BN 4th Infantry Regiment 'Warrior'
2nd BN 30th Infantry Regiment 'Wild Boars'
5th BN 25th Field Artillery Regiment 'Thunder'
Division Artillery 'Mountain Thunder' (HQ only)

The division also has a HQ BN, Aviation BDE and Sustainment BDE	Each BCT has a HQ element, recce element, engineer BN and a support BN

The 10th Mountain Division is the only division of the US Army specialising in mountain warfare. Organised as the 10th Division in July, 1918, World War One ended before it saw combat. On July 10, 1943, the unit received the designation 10th Light Division (Alpine), and occupied Camp Hale, in the Rocky Mountains of Colorado. In World War Two the division fought in Italy, entering combat in January, 1945. Notably, after the war many members of the division, now experienced in skiing and mountaineering, were heavily involved in developing sport and recreational skiing in the United States.

After the war it became a standard infantry division with a training mission until 1954, when it deployed to Germany as part of the American commitment to NATO. In 1958 the unit was deactivated. The army reactivated the 10th Mountain Division in 1985, during a reorganisation period. Stationed at Fort Frum, New York, it was organised as a light infantry unit. Troops from the division saw a deployment to Somalia in 1992. During this mission, the unit provided troops for the quick reaction force which relieved the Rangers during the Battle of Mogadishu, widely known today as the 'Blackhawk Down' incident.

The 10th Mountain was among the first army units to send troops to Afghanistan after the 9/11 attacks on the United States. Battalions and brigades from the unit made frequent deployments to Afghanistan and Iraq during the War on Terror years. More recently, the 10th Mountain has sent troops to Europe to reinforce NATO and to Syria and Iraq as part of Operation Inherent Resolve, the mission against remnants of the so-called Islamic State.

Currently, the division's artillery battalions are still organic to its BCTs. The DIVARTY has training oversight over them. The division's third BCT is stationed at Fort Johnson, Louisiana.

ABOVE LEFT: Cartridge cases and metallic ammunition links fall from this M240 machine gun during a live fire exercise at Fort Drum, New York. (US ARMY)

LEFT: Deployed soldiers from the 10th Mountain Division board a CH-47 helicopter at an undisclosed location in Mid-2024. (US ARMY)

25th Infantry Division

The 25th Infantry Division is stationed at Schofield Barracks, Hawaii. It has a long history and connection to the state of Hawaii, going back to the unit's formation on October 1, 1941. Various units stationed in Hawaii were used to create the division, which went on to fight at Guadalcanal, New Georgia, and the Philippines, earning the nickname 'Tropic Lightning'.

After the war, the division did occupation duty in Japan before fighting in the Korean War, Vietnam, and later in Iraq and Afghanistan. One BCT deployed to Iraq and Syria in 2019 for operations against the so-called Islamic State.

The 25th is the US Army's main division for contingencies in the Pacific region. It has undergone several changes in recent years and has some unusual features. Previously, two of the division's brigades, the 1st and 4th, were stationed in Alaska, as the division needed to be ready to fight anywhere in the Pacific area, including the colder and more mountainous northern regions, including the Korean Peninsula. When the army activated the 11th Airborne Division in Alaska, both those brigades transferred to the new unit. This is why the 25th Division currently has only 2nd and 3rd BCTs.

Both remaining BCTs have two infantry battalions each, instead of the normal three. To compensate for this shortfall, the division has affiliated with two outside infantry battalions who would join the division if needed. The 2nd BCT has the 1st Battalion, 151st Infantry Regiment of the Indiana National Guard. This is not unusual as several active divisions depend on National Guard units to round out their numbers. The 3rd BCT is affiliated with the 100th Infantry Battalion, 442nd Infantry Regiment. It is the only combat unit in the US Army Reserve and descends from the famous 442nd Regiment, which during World War Two was composed of Americans of Japanese ancestry. This unit is spread across the Pacific, with subunits located in Hawaii, Guam, Saipan, American Samoa, and Washington.

25th Infantry Division
2nd Infantry Brigade Combat Team 'Warriors'
1st BN, 21st Infantry Regiment 'Gimlets'
1st BN, 27th Infantry Regiment 'Wolfhounds'
1st BN, 151st Infantry Regiment 'Spartans' (Indiana National Guard)
3rd Infantry Brigade Combat Team 'Broncos'
2nd BN, 27th Infantry Regiment 'Wolfhounds'
2nd BN, 35th Infantry Regiment 'Cacti'
100th BN, 442nd Infantry Regiment 'Go for Broke' (Army Reserve)
Division Artillery 'Tropic Thunder'
2nd BN, 11th Field Artillery Regiment 'On Time'
3rd BN., 7th Field Artillery Regiment 'Never Broken'
125th Intelligence and Electronic Warfare BN

The division also has a HQ BN, Aviation BDE and Sustainment BDE	Each BCT has a HQ element, recce element, engineer BN and a support BN

RIGHT: A machine gunner fires a burst down a road against an attacking force during a training exercise. As an area fire weapon, machine guns are very effective at night, though their muzzle flash can reveal their position. (US ARMY)

BELOW: A team leader directs the fire of his grenadier during an exercise with the Philippine Army for Exercise Salaknib 24 at Fort Magsaysay north of Manila. (US ARMY)

11th Airborne Division

Arctic Angels

The US Army's newest division is the 11th Airborne, headquartered at Joint Base Elmendorf-Richardson in Alaska. The unit dates to World War Two, activated on February 25, 1943. It is less well-known than the airborne divisions that served in Europe, but the 11th performed well during the fighting in the Philippines. This included a quickly planned and very successful rescue of interned US citizens at Los Banos (see page 40). One combat team from the division fought in Korea.

The unit served as a testbed for helicopter tactics in the early 1960s, redesignated the 11th Air Assault Division. Once the testing was successfully concluded, the unit was reflagged as the 1st Cavalry Division. The 11th was officially inactivated in July 1965.

In May 2022, the army reactivated the 11th Airborne Division, assembling it from various units in the former US Army Alaska organisation. This gave these units a common identity and oriented them toward a common combat mission. Two BCTs from the 25th Infantry Division, stationed in Alaska, were assigned to the new division. The 1st Stryker BCT became the 1st Infantry BCT, while the 4th Infantry BCT (Airborne) became the 2nd BCT (Airborne).

A second purpose in creating a new division was developing the capability to fight effectively in Arctic regions. As climate change causes northern ice to melt, new land and resources are exposed for exploitation. This marks the Arctic as a region for conflict in the coming decades.

The new division also has a mission to test and develop new vehicles and equipment for operating in an Arctic environment. The 1st BCT soon turned in its Strykers and is testing the Cold Weather All-Terrain Vehicle, along with new types of cold weather clothing and other items. A unit deployed in the Arctic must sustain itself in a cold and barren climate.

ABOVE: These paratroopers from the 2nd BCT are staged on a C-17 transport just prior to a parachute drop at Donnelly Training Area, Alaska. (US ARMY)

LEFT: A soldier patrols on a snowmobile in an Alaskan forest. His kit is combination of existing issue and new items undergoing field testing. (US ARMY)

11th Airborne Division
1st Infantry Brigade Combat Team ' Arctic Wolves'
1st BN, 5th Infantry Regiment 'Bobcat'
1st BN, 24th Infantry Regiment 'Legion'
2nd BN, 8th Field Artillery Regiment 'Automatic'
2nd Infantry Brigade Combat Team (Airborne) 'Spartans'
1st BN, 501st Infantry Regiment 'Geronimo'
3rd BN, 509th Infantry Regiment 'Stand in the Door'
2nd BN, 377th Field Artillery Regiment 'Spartan Steel'

The division also has a HQ BN, Aviation Command and Sustainment BN	Each BCT has a HQ element, recce element, engineer BN and a support BN

28th Infantry Division

The Iron Division

This National Guard unit is the oldest division in the US Army. It originated in Pennsylvania and that state was the first to organise its combat forces at divisional size. The unit's red keystone insignia and original nickname comes from the state's appellation of the 'Keystone State', due to Pennsylvania's crucial position in the early years of the nation. The shape of the keystone on the badge caused German troops to call the 28th the 'Bloody Bucket' division during World War Two. Today, the division prefers to use an older nickname from World War One, the Iron Division.

The division's combat history spans from the Spanish American War, both World Wars, the Gulf War and the conflicts in Iraq and Afghanistan. This includes service in Operation Inherent Resolve against the so-called Islamic State.

As with the other National Guard divisions, each had its origin in one particular state, larger states which had the population to support division-sized elements. Over time, however, as the Guard has reduced in size, its divisions began to incorporate units from other states, usually neighbouring ones. Though the 28th is still a Pennsylvania unit at its core, it has units from Maryland, Ohio, and New Jersey.

The division's 56th Stryker Brigade was the first Stryker-equipped unit in the National Guard. This unit traces its origins to the 'Associators,' a militia unit raised by Benjamin Franklin in 1747. This makes it one of the United States' oldest military units, and its subordinate battalions possess battle streamers (small ribbons carried on the unit's flag) from most of the wars in American history.

The 28th remains active and regularly sends troops around the United States and the world for various exercises and occasional operations. The Pennsylvania National Guard has an established training partnership with Lithuania and regularly sends troops there.

28th Infantry Division
2nd Infantry Brigade Combat Team
1st BN, 109th Infantry Regiment 'Men of Iron'
1st BN, 110th Infantry Regiment 'Fighting 10th'
1st BN, 175th Infantry Regiment '5th Maryland'
1st BN, 107th Field Artillery Regiment
56th Stryker Brigade Combat Team
1st BN, 111th Infantry Regiment 'Associators'
1st BN, 112th Infantry Regiment
2nd BN, 112th Infantry Regiment
1st BN, 108th Field Artillery Regiment

The division also has a HQ BN, Aviation BDE and Sustainment BDE	Each BCT has a HQ element, recce element, engineer BN and a support BN

29th Infantry Division

Blue and Gray

Headquartered in Virginia and Maryland, the 29th Infantry Division combines units from those states as well as combat and support units from Kentucky, North Carolina, South Carolina, West Virginia, Florida, Arizona, Iowa, and Alabama. It also has administrative and training oversight of the Arkansas National Guard's 142nd Field Artillery Brigade.

The unit is nicknamed the Blue and Gray Division because of its origins in Virginia, a former Confederate state and Maryland, which remained in the Union, during the American Civil War. Union soldiers wore blue and Confederate troops wore grey. When the army activated the division in 1917, the Civil War was still prominent in the American cultural mind; there were still veterans of the war alive and having reunions together. The division's insignia reflects the reconciliation between the two sides; similar to a transposed Yin and Yang, it is a Korean symbol for life with two intertwined teardrops, one in blue, the other in grey. It was the first divisional patch approved by the US Army.

That symbol became famous in military history when the 116th Infantry Regiment went ashore at Omaha Beach on June 6, 1944 alongside the 1st Infantry Division. The division also fought in World War One, did peacekeeping duty in Bosnia in the 1990s, and served in Afghanistan and Iraq.

The division regularly deploys its units to Europe, the Middle East, Africa, and South America for training and deterrence

29th Infantry Division
30th Armored Brigade Combat Team 'Old Hickory'
1st BN, 252nd Armor Regiment
4th BN, 118th Infantry Regiment 'Johnson's Rifles'
1st BN, 120th Infantry Regiment '3rd North Carolina'
1st BN, 113th Field Artillery Regiment 'Axehandles'
53rd Infantry Brigade Combat Team 'Gator'
1st BN, 124th Infantry Regiment 'First Florida'
2nd BN, 124th Infantry Regiment
1st BN, 167th Infantry Regiment '4th Alabama'
2nd BN, 116th Field Artillery Regiment 'Gator Red Legs'
116th Infantry Brigade Combat Team 'Stonewall'
1st BN, 116th Infantry Regiment 'Red Dragon'
3rd BN, 116th Infantry Regiment
1st BN, 149th Infantry Regiment
1st BN, 111th Field Artillery Regiment '1st Virginia Artillery'

The division also has a HQ BN, Aviation BDE and Sustainment BDE

Each BCT has a HQ element, recce element, engineer BN and a support BN

missions. In 2024 it oversaw a river crossing operation (known as a 'wet gap crossing') in Poland as part of the Steadfast Defender 24 exercise, combining UK, US, and Polish troops. In late 2024, several severe weather events occurred in the eastern United States and the 29th activated Guardsmen to assist in the recovery efforts. Units like the 29th Infantry Division have large number of trucks, helicopters and engineer equipment which are all valuable after a natural disaster.

LEFT: Though not as glamorous, disaster relief is a major role for the National Guard. These troops of the 116th Field Artillery distribute water and food to those affected by Hurricane Helene in September 2024. (US ARMY)

BELOW: Soldiers of the 4th Battalion, 118th Infantry Regiment train with their new M7 rifles. They are among the first National Guard troops to receive the new weapon. (US ARMY)

34th Infantry Division

The Red Bull

The 34th Infantry Division is a reinforced division headquartered in Minnesota. Most of its subordinate units come from Minnesota, Iowa, Idaho, Montana, and Oregon, with small numbers of troops from several other states. It exercises administrative control over several other National Guard brigades in other states.

Raised in 1917, the division fought in World War One and later was the first US Army division sent to the European theatre in World War Two. It arrived in Northen Ireland on January 26, 1942. The unit fought in North Africa and Italy. After the war it was inactivated until 1991. Units of the 34th made numerous deployments to Afghanistan and Iraq.

The 34th Infantry Division has a mix of armoured and infantry BCTs. It also currently controls the

116th Cavalry BCT, whose battalions span Idaho, Montana, Nevada, and Oregon. This gives the division control over four BCTs rather than the normal two or three. However, in the event of war, it is likely the 116th or one of the division's other brigades would be assigned to strengthen another division, such as one of the Regular Army's six divisions which currently only have two brigades.

Notably the 34th's mix of armoured and infantry brigades is unusual. Both of the infantry BCTs are standard, non-mechanised infantry units. The battalions in the 1st Armored BCT and the 116th Cavalry are organised

as combined arms battalions. This means they have two tank companies and two mechanised infantry companies in each battalion. The artillery battalions assigned to support these BCTs are equipped with the Paladin 155mm self-propelled howitzer, so they can keep pace with the fast-moving M1 tanks and M2 Bradleys.

In 2024 the division deployed a battalion-sized task force to the Middle East for Operation Spartan Shield, a deterrence force operated by US Central Command. It replaced a similar force from the California National Guard's 40th Infantry Division.

34th Infantry Division
1st Armored Brigade Combat Team
2nd BN, 136th Infantry Regiment (CA) 'King of the Hill'
1st BN, 194th Armor Regiment (CA) 'Remember Bataan'
1st BN, 145th Armor Regiment (CA) 'Steel Panthers'
2nd Infantry Brigade Combat Team
1st BN, 133rd Infantry Regiment 'Ironman'
1st BN, 168th Infantry Regiment 'Lethal'
2nd BN, 135th Infantry Regiment 'To the Last Man'*
32nd Infantry Brigade Combat Team
3rd BN, 126 Infantry Regiment 'Iron'
2nd BN, 127th Infantry Regiment 'Les Terribles'
1st BN, 128th Infantry Regiment 'Les Terribles'
116th Cavalry Brigade Combat Team
1st Squadron, 163rd Cavalry Regiment 'Men, Do Your Duty'
2nd Squadron, 116th Cavalry Regiment 'Snake River'
3rd Squadron, 116th Cavalry Regiment "Snake River'
Division Artillery
1st BN, 125th Field Artillery Regiment 'Faithful'
1st BN, 148th Field Artillery Regiment
1st BN, 194th Field Artillery Regiment 'Thunder'
1st BN, 120th Field Artillery Regiment 'Red Fox'

The division also has a HQ BN, Aviation BDE and Sustainment BDE	Each BCT has a HQ element, recce element, engineer BN and a support BN

CA – Combined Arms BN
*Some sources show 2-135 IN aligned with the 1st ABCT.

35th Infantry Division

Santa Fe Division

Headquartered in Fort Leavenworth, Kansas, the 35th Infantry Division also contains units from Arkansas, Missouri, Oklahoma, Texas, Utah, and Tennessee. Raised in 1917, it fought in both world wars, fighting in France, the Netherlands and Germany during World War Two. It also served in Bosnia in the 1990s, and in Iraq and Afghanistan. The unit's insignia is a Santa Fe cross, which was used to mark the Santa Fe trail, where the division originally trained.

This division is taking part in several army initiatives as part of the service's transformation efforts. It is organised as a standard light infantry division with its artillery battalions centralised in a DIVARTY organisation rather than assigned to individual BCTs. Unusually, one of its infantry battalions, the 2nd Battalion, 134th Infantry Regiment in the Nebraska National Guard, is an airborne unit. Airborne units are rare in the National Guard.

The division is also in the process of adding a 'Protection Brigade' to its organisation. This unit is still being converted from the Missouri National Guard's 110th Maneuver Enhancement Brigade. This unit will contain air defence, chemical, Military Police, engineer, and support battalions and will provide added defensive capabilities to the division. It is likely the unit will change composition over time as the army experiments with new concepts and methods. This brigade is planned to be complete by 2026.

Plans exist to add several other battalion-sized units, also likely for testing and evaluation. These include an intelligence and electronic warfare battalion, engineer battalion, and division cavalry squadron. Currently, BCTs have their own organic cavalry reconnaissance assets, meaning divisions would have to pull assets from their brigades if needed. This will provide the division headquarters with its own dedicated reconnaissance unit. The 35th will also be testing a battalion of the new M10 Booker Mobile Protected Firepower vehicles, which are designed to add supporting firepower to infantry divisions.

35th Infantry Division
39th Infantry Brigade Combat Team
1st BN, 138th Infantry Regiment 'St. Louis' Own'
1st BN, 153rd Infantry Regiment 'First Arkansas'
2nd BN, 153rd Infantry Regiment 'First Arkansas'
45th Infantry Brigade Combat Team
2nd BN, 134th Infantry Regiment (Airborne) 'From the Sky'
1st B BN, 179th Infantry Regiment 'Tomahawks'
1st B BN, 279th Infantry Regiment 'Movin' On'
72nd Infantry Brigade Combat Team
1st BN, 141st Infantry Regiment 'First Texas'
3rd BN, 141st Infantry Regiment 'First Texas'
3rd BN, 138th Infantry Regiment
Division Artillery
1st BN, 133rd Field Artillery Regiment
1st BN, 160th Field Artillery Regiment 'Always Forward'
1st BN, 206th Field Artillery Regiment 'Aleutian'

The division also has a HQ BN, Aviation BDE and Sustainment BDE	Each BCT has a HQ element, recce element, engineer BN and a support BN

The 35th Division also has a new Protection Brigade with five BNs: one each of Air Defence, Chemical, Military Police, Engineer, and Support.
The division is in process of adding a Cavalry Squadron, Engineer BN, Intelligence and Electronic Warfare BN and a Mobile Protected Firepower BN (M10 Booker)

40th Infantry Division

The Sunburst Division

ABOVE: A mortar squad from the Arizona National Guard's 1st Battalion, 158th Infantry Regiment fire a 60mm mortar at an undisclosed location in the Middle East, June 2024. (US ARMY)

The California National Guard's 40th Infantry Division is the major National Guard combat formation for the western United States. It oversees many units from states across that region, including California, Washington, Oregon, Alaska, Utah, Arizona, and New Mexico. Beyond the Continental United States (CONUS), the division is also assigned units from Hawaii and the 1st Battalion, 294th Infantry Regiment from Guam, which is a US territory rather than a state (Both Guam and Puerto Rico have their own National Guard organisations).

Raised in 1917, the division saw no action during World War One, but like the 38th Division saw its personnel distributed to other divisions to replace battle casualties. It was a Pacific division in World War Two, seeing combat on New Britain and in the Philippines. After the war it performed occupation duty in Korea until 1946. The division returned to service for the Korean War. For a time during the Cold War, the unit was redesignated as an armoured division but eventually regained its infantry assignment. It also saw service in Iraq and Afghanistan.

Like many National Guard units, the 40th makes periodic contributions to Operation Spartan Shield, a force in readiness in the Middle East. In 2024 some of the division's troops deployed to Kosovo as part of the ongoing peacekeeping mission there.

With units arrayed along the American west coast and across the Pacific, the 40th Infantry Division is well positioned to take an active role in military operations in that region, joining the three Regular Army divisions (7th, 11th, and 25th) which are also located in the region. However, to maintain the proficiency of its troops, it takes part in deployments worldwide.

40th Infantry Division
29th Infantry Brigade Combat Team
1st BN, 158th Infantry Regiment 'Bushmasters'
1st BN, 294th Infantry Regiment 'Anywhere, Anytime'
1st BN, 297th Infantry Regiment
41st Infantry Brigade Combat Team 'Sunset'
2nd BN, 162nd Infantry Regiment 'Volunteers'
1st BN, 186th Infantry Regiment 'Guardians of the Western Gate'
1st BN, 200th Infantry Regiment
79th Infantry Brigade Combat Team
1st BN, 65th Infantry Regiment 'Borinqueneers'
1st BN, 160th Infantry Regiment '7th California'
1st BN, 184th Infantry Regiment 'Nightstalkers'
Division Artillery
1st BN, 487th Field Artillery Regiment
2d BN, 218th Field Artillery Regiment
1st BN, 143rd Field Artillery Regiment

The division also has a HQ BN, Aviation BDE and Sustainment BDE	Each BCT has a HQ element, recce element, engineer BN and a support BN

ABOVE: A soldier from the 41st BCT takes part in fire phobia training in Germany as his unit prepares for a peacekeeping deployment in Kosovo. The soldier throwing the firebombs is a Slovenian NATO training partner. (US ARMY)

42nd Infantry Division

The Rainbow Division

The 42nd Infantry Division is headquartered in New York state. It gained the unusual nickname 'Rainbow Division' from then-Major Douglas MacArthur. In 1917, he suggested the formation of a division using various Guard units from around the country which had not yet been assigned to any existing divisions. According to the story, Macarthur stated such a unit would stretch across America 'like a rainbow.' The idea was carried out and the 42nd Division combined guard units from 26 states plus the District of Columbia.

The unit took heavy casualties in World War One, so that when the unit's shoulder patch was changed from a half-arc rainbow to a quarter arc, its soldiers said the change symbolised the loss of half the division's troops. The division served in Europe during World War Two and deployed extensively during the wars in Iraq and Afghanistan. It has also activated troops for numerous natural disasters and civil support operations, common for Guard units.

The division is organised along standard lines, with three BCTs and the usual support elements. Two of its BCTs, the 27th and 44th, retain the numbers of World War Two-era divisions which have since been inactivated. Its third BCT, the 86th, is the only mountain infantry BCT in the US Army, with sub-units from Vermont, Colorado, New Hampshire, Maine, Connecticut, and Massachusetts. Two of its infantry battalions trace their lineage to 1636, making them the oldest regiments in the US Army.

Like other Guard units, it has been frequently tasked to provide units for Operations Spartan Shield and Inherent Resolve in the Middle East. The division is scheduled to send more troops to the Middle East for this operation in May 2025. Units of the 44th Infantry BCT were identified as present in Syria in October 2024.

ABOVE: Artillerymen of Battery C, 3rd Battalion, 112th Field Artillery Regiment fire their M777 155mm howitzer during a mission in Syria in October 2024. (US ARMY)

42nd Infantry Division
27th Infantry Brigade Combat Team
1st BN, 69th Infantry Regiment 'Fighting 69th'
2nd BN, 108th Infantry Regiment 'Blood and Iron'
1st BN, 182nd Infantry Regiment 'North Regiment'
44th Infantry Brigade Combat Team
2nd BN, 113th Infantry Regiment '1st New Jersey'
1st BN, 114th Infantry Regiment '3rd New Jersey'
1st BN, 181st Infantry Regiment 'Keep Your Powder Dry'
86th Infantry Brigade Combat Team
1st BN, 102nd Infantry Regiment 'Stand Forth'
1st BN, 157th Infantry Regiment 'Rifles Up'
3rd BN, 172nd Infantry Regiment 'Ascend to Victory'
Division Artillery
1st BN, 258th Field Artillery Regiment 'Ready and Faithful'
3rd BN, 112th Field Artillery Regiment 'To the Utmost'
1st BN, 101st Field Artillery Regiment 'Boston Light Artillery'

The division also has a HQ BN, Aviation BDE and Sustainment BDE	Each BCT has a HQ element, recce element, engineer BN and a support BN

ABOVE: Soldiers from the Vermont National Guard's 3rd Battalion, 172nd Infantry Regiment train with the British Army's 4th Battalion, The Royal Yorkshire Regiment in Germany in June 2024. Note the American troops carrying British L85A3 Rifles. (US ARMY)

Armour

RIGHT: An M1A2 named *Asgard* of 1st Armored Division fires during crew gunnery training. The unit trained Polish tank crews after Poland purchased the Abrams for its forces. (US ARMY)

The armour branch provides the US Army with its heavy hitting power. Tanks, in concert with mechanised infantry, artillery, attack aviation, and close air support have the firepower to smash through enemy defences and into vulnerable rear areas. Their heavy armour protection allows them to absorb blows and minimise losses. Finally, their mobility allows them to move quickly, outflanking enemy positions or formations.

While the army has ample light infantry forces which can perform most missions, armoured forces enable attacks on well-prepared defensive positions and for long, fast movements, so much of the service's combat forces are armoured and mechanised. As the army transforms to meet future threats, it is paying close attention to battlefield developments in Ukraine, the Middle East and elsewhere, to see how armoured forces need to adapt. New threats such as precision munitions, suicide drones, and autonomous systems require new responses.

In many ways these new threats can be reduced through the use of good tactics. Many of the tank losses on the Russian side in Ukraine were due to poor training and tactical handling of their tank units. The US Army stresses training and adaptability in its troops to minimise the new dangers. New electronic warfare and active protection systems will further protect the force.

The Armored Brigade Combat Team (ABCT) is where most of the army's heavy forces are concentrated. The Regular Army has 11 ABCTs while there are five more in the National Guard (one of these is designated as an Armored Cavalry Regiment). Most of these units have Combined Arms Battalions (CABs), which have two tank companies and two mechanised infantry companies.

This method offers advantages. US Army battalions typically form task forces with their assigned companies and any attached elements. Mixing tank and mechanised infantry companies within the same battalion enables a commander to form tank-infantry task forces from their own organic assets. Other assets such as engineers would still have to be attached from other battalions within the BCT.

Army transformation decisions affecting the armour branch through 2029 include the inactivation of 14 light cavalry squadrons to provide resources for new unit types and the creation of four M10 Booker battalions. Recent conflicts have shown that reconnaissance information is increasingly gained by UAS and other means, reducing the perceived need for as many scouting units and personnel.

BELOW: An M1A2 of the 1st Cavalry Division moves alongside a Polish T-72 during a 'Battle of the Tanks' event between NATO allies in July 2024. (US ARMY)

M1 Abrams

Main Battle Tank

ABOVE: Tanks of the 1st Armored Division manoeuvre in the desert at Fort Irwin, California during a rotation at the National Training Center. (US ARMY)

M-1 Abrams	
In service:	1982 – present
Manufacturer:	General Dynamics Land Systems
Unit cost	$12.5m in 2020 dollars (£10,192,017)
Produced	1980 – present
Number built:	Approximately 10,000
Specifications	
Mass:	73.6 tons combat weight, M1A2 SEPv3
Length:	9.77m
Width:	3.7m
Height:	2.4m
Crew:	Four (commander, gunner, loader, driver)
Main armament:	M256 120mm smoothbore cannon
Secondary armament:	One .50 calibre M2HB machine gun at commander's hatch or in a remotely operated station, one coaxial M240 7.62mm machine gun, one M240 7.62mm machine gun at loader's hatch
Engine:	Honeywell AGT1500 Gas Turbine
Operational range:	425km (264 miles)
Maximum speed:	42mph on roads, 30mph cross country

Now in its fifth decade of operation, the M1 Abrams has undergone extensive improvements over the course of its service. That it still ranks among the world's best tanks is a tribute to its excellent design and ability to be periodically upgraded. Along with designs like the UK's Challenger 3, the latest Abrams are the benchmark against which other tank designs are compared.

The latest version of the Abrams is the M1A2 SEPv3 (Systems Enhancement Package version 3). Its list of improvements includes better armour, an auxiliary power unit to run the electronic systems when the engine is shut down, and a counter IED package. It is also more fuel efficient. The manufacturer is building kits to accommodate the Trophy Active Protection System as well. The army is in the process of upgrading existing tanks to this standard.

Another upgrade, the SEPv4, was under development but was cancelled by the army in favour of a new Abrams design, currently called the M1E3. This is to be a new design with a hybrid electric drive, a new main gun with an autoloader, lighter weight, better networking capabilities, and better armour protection. It will also be able to communicate with autonomous vehicles and have lower electromagnetic and thermal signatures. Many of these desired features are based on observations of tank combat in the Ukraine War.

General Dynamic Land Systems, which manufactures the Abrams, recently revealed an advanced prototype called the Abrams X, but it is not known if this meets all the army's desired capabilities. It also features an automated turret with the three-person crew positioned in the hull. The army states it wants a lighter vehicle to lighten the logistical burden, and the current Abrams has reached the limit of what can be achieved.

The army is estimated to have about 600 M1A2 SEPv3s in service. There are another 1,500 M1A2 SEPv2 models in inventory with about 500 of the older M1A1 SA version as well. There are perhaps another 2,000 Abrams tanks of all type in storage, some of which will likely be upgraded to the latest standard until the M1E3 enters service in the early 2030s.

BELOW: The crew of an M1 demonstrates the tank's ability to fire on the move. Note the tracer round just ahead of the barrel. (US ARMY)

M10 Booker

Mobile Protected Firepower

Decades after retiring the M551 Sheridan light tank, the US Army has adopted a replacement, the M10 Booker. However, the army classifies the new vehicle as an Armored Infantry Support Vehicle, not a light tank. This is because it is intended to act much like a World War Two-era assault gun, providing support to infantry units with its 105mm cannon and machine guns. In that conflict, tanks and other armoured fighting vehicles were used to provide firepower to infantry units, proving the concept.

Its targets are the sorts of things that will hold up a light infantry company's advance, such as bunkers, machine gun nests, and other field

M-10 Booker	
In service:	2024 – present
Used by:	US Army
Manufacturer:	General Dynamics Land Systems
Produced	2024 – present
Number to be built:	Initial contract for 96, plans to build 504
Specifications	
Mass:	42 tonnes
Crew:	Four (commander, gunner, loader, driver)
Main armament:	M35 105mm cannon
Secondary armament:	One .50 calibre M2HB machine gun in a remotely operated station, one coaxial M240 7.62mm machine gun
Engine:	800hp MTU 8V199 Diesel
Operational range:	560km (350 miles)
Maximum speed:	45mph

fortifications. As there is always the possibility of enemy armoured vehicles appearing on the battlefield unexpectedly, it has a secondary mission to engage tanks and other enemy fighting vehicles. The 105mm main gun can use all standard NATO ammunition, including armour-piercing types. While the gun may have trouble against some of the latest generation main battle tanks, overall, the Booker's gun would be a threat to almost all of the vehicles it could engage in combat. It has targeting systems similar to the M1 Abrams.

The vehicle is in initial testing and initial low-rate production while the army field-tests it and develops tactics and doctrine. The first unit to be equipped with an M10 test company is the 82nd Airborne. Other divisions in the Regular Army and National Guard will receive M10s and activate their own test companies as new production becomes available in 2025.

Once the vehicle is fully tested and in full production, the army plans to give each light infantry division a battalion of M10s to supports it infantry BCTs. This battalion would be directed by the division headquarters. If these battalions are organised like standard tank units, there will be three companies with 14 tanks each, with four tanks per platoon and two added M10s for the company commander and executive officer. This would allow a division commander to allocate a company of M10s per brigade. This is similar to how such vehicles were used in World War Two, proving some ideas stand the test of time.

Infantry

Follow Me!

Most of the army's combat brigades are organised as infantry and for good reason. They are the basic component of ground forces - ultimately, everything else in the army is there to enable, support, supply and prepare the infantry to perform the role only they can do. They take and hold ground by engaging the enemy at close quarters. Their motto is 'Follow Me' and the infantry branch is known as the Queen of Battle, likely a nod to the superior mobility of the queen on a chessboard. The infantry's symbol is a pair of crossed muskets.

Infantry come in several types, broadening their flexibility. Standard infantry units are often referred to as light infantry because they lack assigned armoured vehicles and to distinguish them from other kinds. They have some motorised transport but carry much of their equipment on their backs. Airborne infantry does much the same, although they also have the ability to make parachute landings. They are also very lightly equipped and will need reinforcement or relief if landed behind enemy lines. The air assault infantry in the 101st Airborne Division (Air Assault), are similar to the paratroopers but use helicopters for movement and resupply.

Mechanised infantry are the heavy hitters, equipped with the M2 Bradley Infantry Fighting Vehicle (IFV). They accompany the tanks in combined arms battalions and fight on foot with the Bradley's cannon, machine gun and TOW missile launcher providing heavy firepower. Stryker brigades use the lighter, eight-wheeled Stryker armoured vehicle in much the same way. The Bradley is better armoured, has better cross-country mobility and more firepower than most Stryker variants, but the Stryker is faster, easier (and cheaper) to maintain, and Stryker brigades are easier to move to a crisis spot.

Whatever their assignment, infantry are similarly armed and equipped: vehicles allow troops to carry more ammunition, food, water, and equipment, extending the time they can stay in the field without resupply. Along these lines, the army is extensively field testing the new Infantry Squad Vehicle (ISV) for issue to light units, with each brigade receiving enough to carry about a battalion. As part of the army's transformation efforts, infantry units are also experimenting with new UAS, autonomous vehicles, and visual augmentation systems. Most of these new systems provide little in the way of new weapons but have vast potential in enabling infantry squaddies to act quickly and decisively on a future battlefield.

ABOVE: An infantry fire team in a support-by-fire position. They are using their machine gun and grenade launcher to provide suppressive fire for another team which is moving to close with their enemy or objective. (US ARMY)

LEFT: The entire army's purpose is to put an infantry soldier in the right place at the decisive moment. The squaddie in the field is young, tired, and dirty, but also aggressive, motivated to succeed and well-trained. (US ARMY)

Bradley Fighting Vehicle

Infantry Fighting Vehicle

The Bradley has been the US Army's primary Infantry Fighting Vehicle (IFV) for over 40 years. The Bradley has the mobility and speed to keep up with the M1 tank, the armour protection to survive many battlefield threats, and the firepower to destroy enemy armour, IFVs or even helicopters. The Bradley is versatile, and there are several variants including a cavalry fighting vehicle, command post, artillery fire support, and air defence vehicles. Its chassis and many of its components are used in other vehicles, including the M109A7, M270 MLRS, and the new AMPV, reducing logistical burdens.

The latest version of the Bradley is the M2A4. It is fully digitised, including a commander's independent viewer, allowing the commander to scan for targets and stay aware of the vehicle's surroundings while under armour and not interfering with the gunner's duties to acquire and engage targets. Other improvements include upgrades to the suspension, tracks, and electrical system. It also adds a larger engine with 75 more horsepower, enabling the Bradley to accelerate from 0-48kph (30mph)

M2 Bradley	
In Service:	1981 - present
Manufacturer:	BAE Systems
Produced	1981 - present
Number built:	7,000+
Specifications (M2A4)	
Unit cost	$2.38m in 2024 dollars (£1,866,741)
Mass:	36.2 tons
Length:	6.55m
Width:	3.6m
Height:	2.98m
Crew:	Three (driver, gunner, commander)
Main armament:	25mm M242 Bushmaster chain gun, twin launcher for BGM71 TOW missile
Secondary armament:	One coaxial 7.62mm M240 machine gun
Engine:	675hp Cummins VTA-903T diesel
Operational range:	483km (300 miles)
Maximum speed:	66kph (41mph)

in 22 seconds, respectable for such a heavy vehicle. There is an active protection system called Iron Fist under development for the M2A4.

Bradleys have proven effective in combat during the 1991 Gulf War, operations in the Balkans during the 1990s, and during the war in Iraq.

In Ukraine they are one of the more effective IFVs on the battlefield, and when handled well have even taken on Russian main battle tanks. About 300 have been supplied to Ukraine and while they are older models, they have performed well and are popular with their operators. Around a third of them have been destroyed, damaged, or captured, but this is to be expected on a battlefield with the intensity seen in Ukraine where UAS are common, and air superiority doesn't exist.

The US Army has about 6,000 Bradleys, with 2,000 of those in storage. In late 2024 the Army signed a $440m contract with BAE Systems to produce 200 new M2A4s. While a programme to develop a replacement is underway, it is years from production. That vehicle will likely be capable of autonomous operations. Until then, the M2A4 will continue in service for at least another decade.

RIGHT: Under a leaden sky, a TOW missile flashes from the launch tube of an M2A4 Bradley of the 3rd Infantry Division during a firepower demonstration in Latvia. (US ARMY)

BELOW: A company of Bradley IFVs form a convoy at Fort Stewart, Georgia, with an armoured bridgelayer behind them. The various bits of kit hung from the vehicle's side can actually help break up its outline at a distance. (US ARMY)

Stryker

Versatile wheeled armoured vehicle

The Stryker Brigades are the US Army's medium-weight option, between the heavy armoured BCTs and the light infantry units. As a wheeled vehicle, Strykers are less well armed and armoured than the Abrams and Bradleys and their cross-country performance is less than that of tracked vehicles. However, on terrain it can traverse, the Stryker is fast. As a wheeled vehicle it is easier and cheaper to maintain along with being more fuel efficient.

In Iraq and Ukraine, they have proven effective; while they can be damaged and destroyed like any other armoured vehicle, Strykers can absorb damage, especially from mines and IEDs and keep their crew uninjured. Their V-shaped hull dissipates some of the blast of mines and IEDs while their tyres can remain usable even after damage from shrapnel or bullets. There are several examples of Strykers losing one or two road wheels and remaining mobile. About 400 Strykers have been transferred to Ukraine and about 30 are believed to have been destroyed, damaged, or captured.

The Stryker is also versatile, able to be adapted to various roles

M1126 Stryker	
In service:	2002 - present
Manufacturer:	General Dynamics Land Systems
Unit cost	$5m (£4,361,075)
Produced	2001 - present
Number built:	4,900
Specifications	
Mass:	16.47 tons
Length:	6.95m (22ft 10in)
Width:	2.72m (8ft 11in)
Height:	2.64m (8ft 8 in)
Crew:	Two (driver and commander) plus nine troops in the infantry carrier
Main armament:	One .50-cal. Machine gun or one 40mm MK19 grenade launcher
Engine:	Caterpillar 3126 (350hp)
Operational range:	532km (330 miles)
Maximum speed:	96.5kph (62mph)
Variants	M1126 Infantry Carrier M1127 Reconnaissance Vehicle M1128 Mobile Gun System (retired) M1129 Mortar Carrier M1130 Commander's Vehicle M1131 Fire Support Vehicle* M1132 Engineer Squad Vehicle M1133 Medical Evacuation Vehicle M1134 Anti-Tank Missile Vehicle (TOW) M1135 NBC** Reconnaissance Vehicle M1296 Dragoon IFV w/30mm gun turret Short Range Air Defense Vehicle Mobile Experimental High-Energy Laser

*Carries forward artillery observers
**Nuclear-Biological-Chemical

beyond just a personnel carrier. This allows a Stryker BCT to have a common vehicles for multiple roles, simplifying training and maintenance. See the accompanying table on this page for a list of Stryker variants. Of note, the US Army is using the Stryker as a carrier for its new short-range air defence vehicle called M-SHORAD. It carries a 30mm cannon and up to eight Stinger missiles. Many have the ability to carry four stingers and two Hellfire missiles, but in 2024 the army began replacing the Longbow launcher with another Stinger pod. The vehicle is named the Sergeant Stout, after the only US Army air defence soldier to win the Medal of Honor.

The army is experimenting with the Mobile Experimental High-Energy Laser, mounted on a Stryker vehicle. This testbed has a laser and other counter-UAS systems, such as electronic warfare devices and jammers, for defence against various types of drones. As the technology improves it has been upgraded with more powerful lasers.

LEFT: Strykers from the 2nd Armored Cavalry Regiment prepare to dismount infantry during the DEFENDER 24 exercise in Poland. (US ARMY)

LEFT: Armour-piercing rounds fly downrange from a Stryker Dragoon's 30mm cannon during a firepower demonstration in Lithuania. (US ARMY)

Mortars

in the battalion mortar platoon in the headquarters company. Stryker units have a mix of different calibre mortars, some of which are mounted in the vehicles, and some are carried to be operated dismounted. Armoured and combined arms battalions have a platoon of vehicles with 120mm weapons in the battalion mortar platoon.

Mortars provide firepower for infantry units. While less powerful and shorter ranged than artillery, mortars are lighter, more portable and have high rates of fire. They also fire at high angles, allowing them to hit targets behind hills or other cover. Light infantry companies have 60mm mortars in their weapons platoon. The 81mm mortars are

US Mortar Systems			
Specification	60mm M224	81mm M252	120mm M120
Weight	21.1kg (47lb)	41.3kg (91lb)	144.7kg (318lb)
Crew	3	5	5
Sustained ROF*	20 rpm**	16 rpm	4 rpm
Maximum ROF	30 rpm	30 rpm	16 rpm
Range	70-3,490m (76-3,816yds)	91-5,935m (99-6,490yds)	200-7,200m (218-7,874yds)

*ROF: Rate of Fire   **RPM: Rounds Per Minute

RIGHT: A mortar crew from the 2nd Armored Cavalry Regiment fire their 60mm M224 mortar during an exercise in Lithuania. (US ARMY)

BELOW RIGHT: A 1st Armored Division soldier prepares to fire a 120mm round in an M1064 mortar carrier during a live fire in South Korea. (US ARMY)

BELOW: An infantryman from the Maryland National Guard awaits the order to fire an illumination round from an 81mm mortar. Another illumination round burns in the background. (US ARMY)

Small Arms

Tools of a deadly trade

ABOVE: A soldier tests the new M250 light machine gun in Arctic conditions. It fires a new 6.8mm round with better power and penetration than the standard 5.56mm munition. (US ARMY)

ABOVE LEFT: A Stryker crewman fires a burst from the vehicle's 7.62mm M240. The M240 is the US Army's standard general purpose machine gun, carried by infantry and mounted in vehicles from trucks to tanks to helicopters. (US ARMY)

LEFT: Shotguns are usually used for breaching doorways and structures but also have anti-personnel roles. This engineer officer trains with the 12-gauge Mossberg M500. (US ARMY)

BELOW: Paratroopers firing an M3 Multirole Anti-Armor Anti-personnel Weapon (MAAW). Nicknamed the Gustaf or Charlie G, it gives an infantry squad heavy firepower. (US ARMY)

Multiple Launch Rocket Systems

Steel rain

Common Rocket and Missile ammunition		
Type	**Warhead**	**Range (km)**
M26	644 DPICM submunitions	32
M26A2 ER	518 DPICM submunitions	45
M28	Unarmed practice rocket	9
M30 Guided	404 DPICM submunitions	92
M30A1	182,000 tungsten fragments	92
M31 Guided	200lb unitary	92
M39 ATACMS	950 bomblets	165
M39A1 ATACMS	300 bomblets	300
M48 ATACMS	500lb unitary	300
M57 ATACMS	500lb unitary	300
PrSM	200lb tungsten fragments	500

The M270 Multiple Launch Rocket System (MLRS) is the US Army's legacy long range rocket and missile artillery system. It shares a chassis and some automotive components with the Bradley IFV, simplifying logistics. Its armour can withstand small arms and shrapnel. Artillery soldiers refer to the M270 as a Self-Propelled Loader/Launcher (SPLL), pronounced 'Spill'.

Each SPLL has an armoured box launcher behind the crew cab, which holds two ammunition pods. Each pod holds six rockets or one Army Tactical Missile System (ATACMS) missile. The new Precision Strike Missile (PrSM) is more effective than the ATACMS but smaller - two fit in each pod.

These munitions can carry a solid warhead, called a unitary, or hundreds of explosive submunitions. The M30A1 guided rocket has been used in Ukraine with a warhead which sprays the target with 182,000 tungsten fragments. This warhead is devastating to artillery positions, command posts, supply dumps, and other critical targets. The new Ground-Launched Small Diameter Bomb (GLSDB) can be fitted to an MLRS rocket. It has also seen use in Ukraine, with mixed results. While the US has not supplied any M270s to Ukraine, other NATO members including the UK have transferred 16, with none yet reported lost.

The trend with MLRS and HIMARS has been to use precision unitary warhead munitions to limit collateral damage. The army has been in the process of discarding the older submunition equipped rockets and

Multiple Launch Rocket Systems		
	M270A2	**M142**
In service:	1983 to present	2005 to present
Manufacturer:	Lockheed Martin	Lockheed Martin
Produced:	1982 to 2003	2005 to present
Number built:	385 in US Army service	363+ in US Army service
Specifications:		
Mass:	25,000kg (55,100lb)	16, 239kg (35,800lb)
Length:	6.85m (22ft 6in)	7m (23ft)
Width:	2.97m (9ft 9in)	2.4m (7ft 10in)
Height:	2.59m (8ft 6in)	3.2m (10ft 6in)
Crew:	Three (commander, gunner, driver)	Three (commander, gunner, driver)
Armament:	Two rocket/missile pods	One rocket/missile pod
Engine:	Cummins Diesel Engine with 600 hp in M270A2	Caterpillar Diesel Engine with 290 hp
Operational range:	480km (298 miles)	483km (300 miles)
Maximum speed:	64kph (40mph) on roads	94kph (58mph) on roads

missiles due to problems with the dud rate on the bomblets. However, it is does not appear they have all been destroyed, since some have reportedly been supplied to Ukraine during the present war. As the new threat of large-scale conflict with peer opponents looms, there may be no choice but to retain the older ammunition type for the simple reason that it is very effective.

The M270 first saw combat during the 1991 Gulf War, where its punishing, deadly barrages caused Iraqi troops to nickname it 'Steel Rain'. Since then, the design continues in service with several upgrades. The latest model is the M270A2. Improvements include a new 600hp engine with a stronger transmission and better armour for the crew cabin. Most importantly, the vehicle has a new fire control system so it can use the new PrSM.

The US Army's other MLRS system is the wheeled M142 High Mobility Artillery Rocket System (HIMARS). The army developed this version to answer the need for a lighter and more easily transportable MLRS. The M142 can be carried aboard a C-130 aircraft. It is not as well protected as the M270 and cannot cross rough terrain like its tracked predecessor. However, it is easier and less expensive to maintain and uses considerably less fuel. The simpler maintenance needs have led to the M142 having a very high operational readiness rate. It is also faster on roads; its lower mobility on rough terrain has generally not proven a hindrance in service.

HIMARS saw combat service in Iraq, Afghanistan, and Syria. They continue to see use in the Middle East as part of Operation Inherent Resolve and Task Force Spartan. The US supplied 39 to Ukraine and it is believed two have been destroyed and two damaged. The M142 has proven very effective in both the Middle East and Ukraine, though the Russians have developed countermeasures to guided MLRS rockets that make them less accurate.

HIMARS success on the battlefield and its lower operational costs have generated interest in adopting it among a dozen nations beyond the eight countries which already use it. HIMARS is further capable of upgrades which will keep it in frontline service for at least another decade.

LEFT: American and Jordanian HIMARS launchers carry out a live fire during Exercise Eager Lion 24. (US ARMY)

BELOW: An M270 on exercise in Germany. In this case the purple smoke simulates an unexpected chemical attack, compelling the crew to take countermeasures. (US ARMY)

M109A7 Paladin

Self-propelled artillery

The M109 series has been the US Army's primary self-propelled 155mm howitzer since the 1960s and the latest versions will continue to serve for decades more. The design's longevity is due to its simple, rugged design, reliability and most importantly, the ability to absorb technological upgrades. It is the service's only self-propelled cannon.

The latest version of the Paladin is the M109A7. It shares many components with the Bradley IFV, including the tracks, transmission, and engine. This allows the vehicle to handle higher weights: the Paladin can absorb over 10,000kg in future weight increases without stressing the chassis. This allows for considerable armour and weapons upgrades if needed.

The hydraulic system on previous models is replaced with a more powerful and faster electric version. The electrical system is overbuilt to accommodate future increases in power needs. This electrical system allows the Paladin's automatic gun rammer to seat the projectile and powder charges more consistently, which increases accuracy by ensuring more uniform velocities for each round.

Each 155mm shell weighs 43.2kg and has a lethal radius of at least 50m depending on shell type. The Paladin can fire at a maximum rate of four rounds per minute for three minutes before the crew must slow down to avoid overheating the cannon. The sustained rate of fire is one round per minute.

The older M109A6 Paladin is still in service as well but is gradually being replaced by the M109A7. In 2024 the US Army signed a $493m contract with BAE Systems to build an undisclosed number of Paladins, including the M992A3 Field Artillery Ammunition Supply Vehicle (FAASV). Normally, one FAASV accompanies each Paladin to carry additional ammunition and equipment. It is built on the same chassis and externally resembles a Paladin without its cannon mounted. It carries 95 rounds of ammunition for the Paladin.

Paladins are usually organised into battalions of 18 guns, divided into three firing batteries with six guns each. The firing batteries are divided into two platoons of three guns each. For battery defence each Paladin carries an M2 .50-calibre machine gun atop its turret while the FAASV carries a Mk.19 40mm grenade launcher. The 155mm cannon can also be used to directly fire at close targets.

M109A7 Paladin	
In Service:	2015 - present
Manufacturer:	BAE Systems
Produced:	2015 - present
Number built:	310 with more on order
Specifications	
Mass:	35,000kg (78,000lb)
Length:	9.7m
Width:	3.9m
Height:	3.3m
Crew:	Four (driver, gunner, loader, section chief/commander)
Main armament:	M284A2 155mm howitzer
Secondary armament:	One roof-mounted .50-caliber M2HB machine gun
Engine:	Cummins VTA-903T diesel (675hp)
Operational range:	300km (186 miles)
Maximum speed:	61kph (38mph)

Towed Cannon

Guns for Stryker and light infantry units

The US Army's two towed howitzer systems are the 155mm M777A2 and M119A3 105mm cannon. These weapons provide the heavy punch for the service's Stryker and light infantry brigades. Towed weapons are lighter and easier to maintain than self-propelled guns, but they lack armour protection, require a vehicle to move them, and take longer to emplace and displace, making them more vulnerable to UAS and counterbattery fire.

The M777A2, nicknamed the 'Triple 7', is often referred as a lightweight howitzer due to the use of titanium in its components, reducing overall weight. It can be towed by medium trucks of 2.5 US tons capacity or greater. M777s can also be sling-loaded by the CH47 Chinook helicopter. It can be emplaced in three minutes and displaced in the same amount of time. The M777A2 is distinguished by its digital fire control system, upgraded software, and the ability to fire precision munitions such as the Excalibur guided round.

The M119A3 is the latest variant of this long-serving 105mm howitzer, a license-built copy of the British L119. This version has a digital fire control system, an improved recoil mechanism and better durability in cold weather environments. It is light enough to be towed by a Humvee and can be sling loaded by the UH60 or CH47 helicopters. The weapon can be parachute dropped for airborne operations, making it one of the most powerful weapons an airborne unit will have available if it is dropped behind the front lines. The M119 is easy to use and maintain and has a high maximum rate of fire. It is well-suited to use by airborne and air assault units.

Both types have been used in conflicts in the Middle East and supplied to Ukraine. Due to a towed weapon's lower mobility and lack of protection, many have been damaged or destroyed in that conflict, often by Russian Lancet suicide drones or UAS-directed artillery fire.

Towed artillery battalions have two batteries of M119s with six guns each, and one six-gun battery of M777s. Some airborne battalions have only one of the M119 batteries. An artillery battalion in divisions with Stryker BCTs have three batteries of M777s with six guns each. Some National Guard battalions may have three batteries with four guns each.

US Army Towed Howitzers		
	M777A2 155mm	**M119A3 105mm**
In service:	2005 to present	1989 to present
Manufacturer:	BAE Systems	Rock Island Arsenal, Illinois
Produced:	2000 to present	1989 to present
Number built	1,300 to present	1,000 in U.S. service (all types)
Specifications		
Mass:	4,200kg (9,300lb)	1,936kg
Length:	10.7m (35ft) when deployed for firing	8.8m (28ft 10in)
Crew	Five to eight personnel	Five to seven personnel
Rate of fire:	Two rounds per minute (sustained) Five rounds per minute (maximum)	Three rounds per minute (sustained) Eight rounds per minute (maximum)
Maximum firing range	22.5km (14 miles) standard; 30km (19 miles) using rocket assisted projectile (RAP); 40km (25 miles) using Excalibur guided round	17,500m (19,138yd) /19,500m (21,325yd) using rocket assisted projectile (RAP)

LEFT: A gun crew of the 2nd Armored Cavalry Regiment fire their M777 howitzer at Grafenwoehr, Germany. Stryker units use the M777 exclusively. (US ARMY)

LEFT: Smoke billows after California National Guardsmen fire their M119 in direct fire mode against a close ground target. (US ARMY)

Aviation

The aviation branch operates the US Army's fleet of aircraft. The army has a small force of fixed-wing aircraft, mostly small transports, and electronic warfare/surveillance platforms. However, the vast majority of army aircraft are helicopters, organised into combat aviation brigades (CAB). Each division has a CAB and there are independent CABs to serve as corps and army level assets.

CABs generally have two attack/reconnaissance battalions with 48 AH64 Apaches and a dozen UAS. An assault battalion has 30 UH60 Blackhawks for troop and cargo transport while the general support battalion has 12 CH47 Chinooks and 23 Blackhawks for heavy lift, medical evacuation, and command and control. CABs in the National Guard fly the UH72 Lakota and some CABs lack some battalions.

The army's transformation plans extend to its CABs. They are to be reorganised into light and heavy CABs, with four light CABs for the 10th Mountain, 25th Infantry, 82nd, and 101st Airborne divisions. The rest of the divisions (except 11th Airborne) will get a heavy CAB. The 11th Airborne currently has an Arctic aviation command with two battalions rather than a CAB.

The heavy CABs will lose some of their UH60s, which will be added to the light CABs. The 101st, as an air assault division, will get an extra battalion of CH47s to improve its lift capabilities. These changes apply to Regular Army divisions; it is not clear what changes will be made in National Guard and Army Reserve units. These modifications aim to make the CABs more flexible and capable for the division they serve. The new targeting and communication technologies the army is experimenting with will also enable army attack aviation to respond more quickly in the targeting cycle.

Unique in the army's aviation community is the 160th Special Operations Aviation Regiment (SOAR), which provides helicopter support to special forces units throughout the US military. This unit flies modified Blackhawks and Chinooks along with AH6/MH6 Little Birds, nicknamed the 'killer egg' due to its distinctive hull shape. This unit has its own entrance qualification and puts its prospective members through a specialised training course to prepare them to service in the unit.

RIGHT: A soldier signals a UH60 which is hovering over an MLRS rocket pod in preparation to pick it up for sling load transport to a unit in the field. This image is of an undisclosed location in the Middle East. (US ARMY)

AH 64 Apache

Attack helicopter

The AH64 Apache has been in frontline US Army service for nearly 40 years. The design is older than many of the pilots flying it. Despite its overall age, a series of upgrades have kept the AH64 competitive and lethal in the current combat environment. Originally designed to destroy Soviet armour in the Cold War, the Apache is heavily armed, armoured to protect the crew and vital systems from up to 23mm cannon fire, and fitted with the latest digital and tactical data systems.

The latest version of the Apache is the AH64E. It has a data system which allows it to communicate and exchange digital information with other air and ground systems. It has a more powerful engine than its predecessor giving a higher speed and has composite rotor blades, better landing gear, and better ability to operate from naval vessels, useful for the Pacific theatre. The AH64E is also more fuel efficient, allowing it to stay aloft for longer, on station and in support of ground troops or transport helicopter movements. The crew can use their digital systems to control UAS, and each attack helicopter battalion has a dozen UAS, with another 12 in the combat aviation brigade.

The AH-64E can be equipped with the Longbow targeting radar in a radome above the rotors. Usually, only a few helicopters per company carry them, as they can share target data with the rest of the unit. The radar is heavy, about 500lb, and reduces the aircraft's weapon or fuel load, so it is impractical and overly redundant to entirely equip a unit with them.

AH-64s operate in attack weapons teams (AWT) of two or more helicopters. Whenever possible they make use of UAS for extended reconnaissance and target location. Armament will vary depending on mission but is usually a mix of Hellfire missiles and 2.75in rockets, though the Apache can use the Spike and Maverick missiles as well as the air-to-air version of the Stinger missile.

Apache units spend most of their time supporting ground troops. They fly low and fast to minimise exposure, using terrain features such as hills and forests to mask their location. Using cover such as trees, hills, or buildings, they use UAS or the Longbow radar to locate targets.

The helicopter will emerge from cover to fire before returning to cover and then moving before launching another attack.

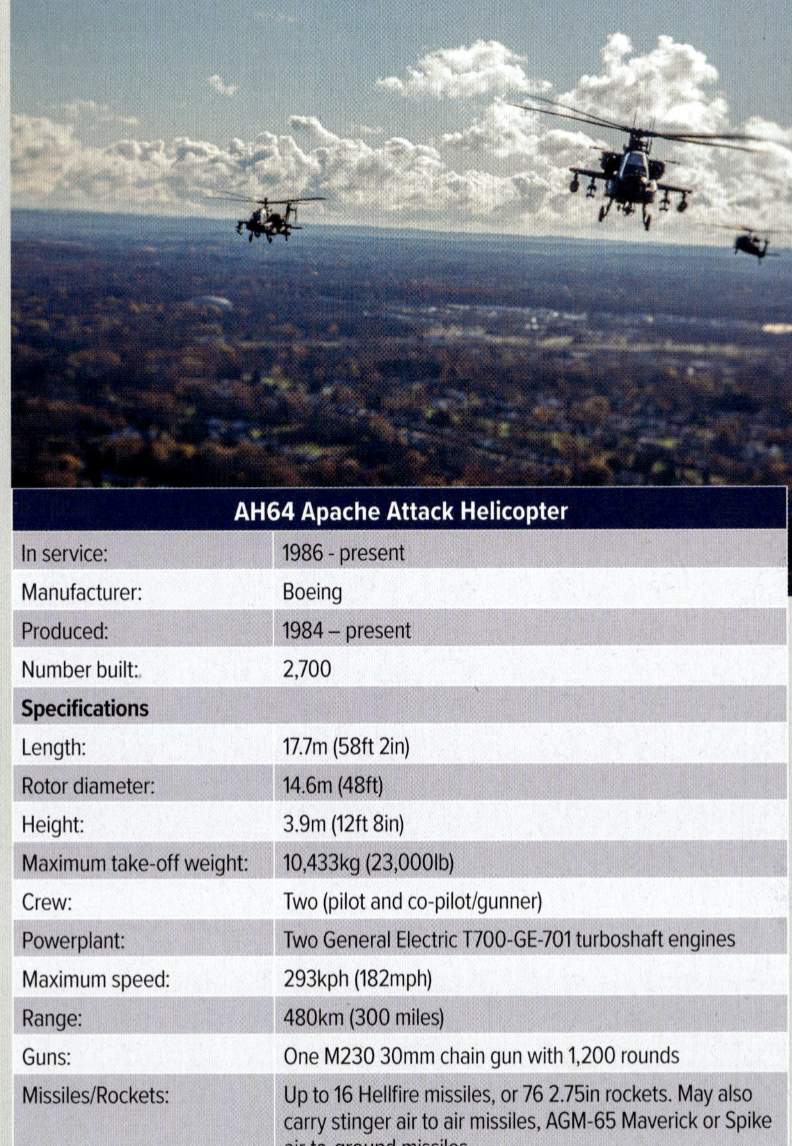

AH64 Apache Attack Helicopter	
In service:	1986 - present
Manufacturer:	Boeing
Produced:	1984 – present
Number built:	2,700
Specifications	
Length:	17.7m (58ft 2in)
Rotor diameter:	14.6m (48ft)
Height:	3.9m (12ft 8in)
Maximum take-off weight:	10,433kg (23,000lb)
Crew:	Two (pilot and co-pilot/gunner)
Powerplant:	Two General Electric T700-GE-701 turboshaft engines
Maximum speed:	293kph (182mph)
Range:	480km (300 miles)
Guns:	One M230 30mm chain gun with 1,200 rounds
Missiles/Rockets:	Up to 16 Hellfire missiles, or 76 2.75in rockets. May also carry stinger air to air missiles, AGM-65 Maverick or Spike air-to-ground missiles

ABOVE: A pair of Apaches fly over a town in the US, followed by a UH60 Blackhawk. They are on their way to do a flyover at a football game! (US ARMY)

BELOW: An Apache fires a pair of 2.75in rockets during NATO training in Poland. This helicopter was helping train joint terminal air controllers of the Polish Army, who help direct attack helicopters in combat. (US ARMY)

Air Defence Artillery

ABOVE: Two Sergeant Stout air defence vehicles enter a training range in Germany. That day's event involved shooting the system's 30mm and 7.62mm weapons. (US ARMY)

The air defence artillery (ADA) branch of the US Army specialises in anti-aircraft operations of all types, from enemy aircraft to UAS, rockets, missiles, and even incoming artillery and mortar rounds. Due to the lack of a serious aerial threat during the wars in Iraq and Afghanistan, the ADA atrophied as the focus went to more vital capabilities. The army knew this was an issue but had little choice but to make that trade-off during those conflicts. Now, with the focus again on potential opponents with significant aerial strength, the ADA is being restored to its former strength with abilities at all levels.

At the tactical level, ADA units use the Avenger, a Humvee mounting a .50-calibre machine gun and eight Stinger missiles. While effective, it is growing obsolete and lacks armour protection. It is being replaced by the Maneuver – Short Range Air Defense (M-SHORAD), based on the Stryker armoured vehicle. This vehicle was recently named the Sergeant Stout, after a Medal of Honor recipient. It is better protected than the Humvee and carries a 30mm cannon, 7.62mm machine gun, a box launcher for four Stingers and another for two Hellfire missiles. The Hellfire launcher has some problems and is being replaced by another four-round Stinger launcher. Another Stryker variant uses a laser to engage targets - while still in testing, it appears promising.

The Patriot missile (see page 103) occupies the next echelon and is the US Army's main air defence missile system.

The Terminal High Altitude Area Defense (THAAD) system is the army's anti-ballistic missile weapon. Paired with an advanced radar called the AN/TPY2 ('Tippy 2'), THAAD can hit missiles either inside or outside the atmosphere. THAAD has proven successful in extensive testing and one combat use by the UAE, which shot down a Houthi ballistic missile in 2022.

There are seven THAAD batteries with another funded and under construction. These units have been strategically placed in critical spots around the globe, including the Pacific, Europe, Saudi Arabia, and South Korea. In late 2024 a THAAD battery deployed to Israel to provide protection against Iranian ballistic missiles.

Army transformation efforts place heavy focus on the ADA. A recent army white paper summarised new investments, including four more Indirect Fire Protection Capability (IFPC) battalions. Other measures include giving air defence battalions a counter-UAS battery and creating four more M-SHORAD battalions. These plans reveal how serious the US Army is about creating integrated air and missile defence systems, particularly at the division and corps levels.

RIGHT: Three THAAD launchers set up at Fort Cavazos, Texas. THAAD units are in high demand and must be ready for deployments at short notice. (US ARMY)

MIM-104 Patriot

Long-serving surface-to-air missile

The Mobile Interceptor Missile (MIM) -104 Patriot is a long-serving weapon, entering service in 1984 as the US Army's medium range Surface to Air Missile (SAM). Patriot is actually an acronym for the system's radar, 'Phased Array Tracking Radar to Intercept On Target.' It has received regular upgrades to keep it capable on 21st century battlefields.

Initially intended as an anti-aircraft weapon, upgraded Patriot missiles are effective against UAS, loitering munitions, ballistic, and cruise missiles. Upgraded versions go by the acronym PAC (Patriot Advanced Capability). PAC-1 and PAC-2 missiles give varying levels of capability against ballistic missiles, while the PAC-3 is substantially redesigned to make it more effective against ballistic missiles. It provides a hit-to-kill ability, where it destroys the incoming target by physically striking it.

A Patriot battery typically consists of a radar, control station, generator vehicle, support, and ammunition trucks and six to eight launchers, each of which carries four to 16 missiles, depending on type. The battery is divided into headquarters, maintenance, fire control and launcher platoons. The most modern systems can only fire the PAC-2 or PAC-3 missiles. Launchers can be sited up to 10km from the radar, making the system harder to attack and increasing the area a battery can defend. A Patriot battalion has a headquarters, maintenance company and four to six firing batteries.

Patriot was first used in the 1991 Gulf War, where its success rate against Iraqi Scud missiles is still a matter of debate. Improvement programmes steadily improved the Patriot, and its success rate climbed steadily during subsequent conflicts. Patriot units are among the most frequently deployed units in the US Army, with those deployments being longer than average for American units.

The US, Germany, and the Netherlands donated Patriot batteries to Ukraine, giving the weapon its longest and heaviest combat use. It has been used to shoot down aircraft, ballistic, and cruise missiles, UAS and an unconfirmed number of Russian Kinzhal hypersonic missiles. In at least one intercept of a Kinzhal, several missiles were fired from different launchers to ensure an intercept. It is simpler and easier to use than comparable Russian SAMs.

"Patriot has prove[n] to be a very reliable system," said Ben Hodges, a retired three-star general who commanded US Army forces in Europe following Russia's annexation of Crimea. "The Ukrainians learned very quickly how to operate it, and even more impressively they learned very quickly how to employ it to great effect."

The US Army is also working on how best to integrate the Patriot with the THAAD for theatre air defence.

MIM-104 Patriot Missile System Characteristics	
Country of origin	United States
Crew	Three
Maximum range	105km (65.2 miles) MIM-104A 160km (99.4 miles) MIM-104D/E PAC-2 80km (49.7 miles) MIM-104F PAC-3 (Aircraft target) 40km (24.8 miles) MIM-104F PAC-3 (Ballistic missile target)
Maximum firing altitude	18.3km (11.3 miles) MIM-104A 32km (19.8 miles) MIM-104D/E PAC 2 24km (14.9 miles) MIM-104F PAC-3 (Aircraft target) 20km (12.4 miles) MIM-104F PAC-3 (Ballistic missile target)
Maximum speed	PAC-3: 6,170kph (3,830mph)
Missiles	Four-16 per launcher, six to eight launchers in a battery
Warhead	PAC-2: 90kg Blast-Fragmentation PAC-3: Hit to Kill (HTK) vehicle

ABOVE: A Patriot battery at an undisclosed location in the Middle East, set up to intercept ballistic and cruise missiles. (US ARMY)

BELOW: A Patriot missile flies from its launcher during an exercise in New Mexico with allies from the Netherlands Air Defence Command. (US ARMY)

FIM92 Stinger

Portable air defence

The FIM92 Stinger is the US Army's Man-Portable Air Defense System (MANPADS). The weapon entered service in 1978 and like most long-enduring Cold War weapons systems, has undergone extensive upgrades to maintain its effectiveness. The system is intended for battlefield use by combat troops, with two-soldier air defence teams allocated to each battalion within a division. Their original use was against enemy helicopters and low-flying strike aircraft, though the weapon has proven able to engage UAS on the 21st century battlefield.

Two soldiers normally operate the Stinger, though one can do so if needed. It uses infrared guidance, homing on the heat signature of a target. Early MANPADS had difficulty engaging an aircraft from anywhere except the rear, where the infrared signature was greatest. However, Stinger can be fired at a target from any aspect: after launch it tracks the target's airframe rather than the hot exhaust.

The Stinger first saw combat in the 1982 Falklands conflict, covertly issued to British SAS troops, who reportedly downed several aircraft with them. The weapon's fame, however, came in Afghanistan during the 1980s, when the US supplied them to the Afghan mujahideen fighting the Soviet invasion. Though the provision of Stingers received extensive media coverage at the time, its actual effectiveness is debated.

More recently, the Stinger is in use in Ukraine, where it has been reasonably effective. Exact numbers are undisclosed, but the US and several NATO nations provided several thousand missiles to Ukraine. While the Ukrainians have downed a number of aircraft and UAS with the Stinger, some troops have complained their missiles malfunctioned, apparently because they were from old stocks which were past their shelf life. Like any missile system, they do require occasional maintenance to remain operational.

The Ukraine War compelled the resumption of Stinger production due to the number of missiles supplied to that nation. There were production problems because some of the components were obsolete and unobtainable, requiring new designs to replace them. Nevertheless, Stinger production is underway again, albeit at a reduced rate.

The Stinger is a versatile weapon, with a vehicle mounted version in use on the Avenger and M-SHORAD air defence vehicles in US Army use. There is also an air-to-air version of the Stinger which can be mounted on helicopters, including the AH64 Apache.

FIM92 Stinger	
Origin	US
Length	152cm (59.9in)
Weight	15.7kg (34.6lb)
Target ceiling	3.5km (2.17 miles)
Range	4.5km (2.8 miles)
Speed	Mach 2.54
Warhead	1kg (2.2lb) HE

Infantry Squad Vehicle

New mobility vehicle in field test with light infantry units

Light infantry units can be moved to a battlefield quickly. Once they are there, however, they can only move as fast as they can walk and must carry all their kit and rations on their backs. The Infantry Squad Vehicle (ISV) is an answer to that problem, though a controversial one to some.

The ISV is based on the Chevrolet Colorado ZR2 pickup, popular in the United States' civilian market for its off-road capabilities. Fully 90% of the ISV's components are available on the civilian market. The intent is a vehicle which is easy to maintain and repair and provides mobility to an infantry squad. It can also carry the squad's kit, along with extra ammunition, food, and water, extending the time the squad can go before needing resupply.

The vehicle does have critics, who decry the vehicle's lack of armour and armament. The ISV did have some drivetrain problems during earlier testing as well, although the army states it has made changes to eliminate those issues. The army also stresses that this is a transport vehicle, not a fighting vehicle. It is not intended that soldiers would fight from it. Rather, the ISV acts more as a 'battle taxi'. It carries its squad close to the battle area, where they disembark and move out on foot. The vehicle can remain behind and be on hand for resupply or casualty evacuation.

Currently the vehicle is fielded with the 82nd and 101st Airborne divisions, where it is being extensively field tested. It has been used by the 101st in several army transformation-related exercises to determine its utility and shortcomings in active use. ISVs were also used in disaster relief operations after Hurricane Helene in October 2024.

While pintle and swivel mounts are available for mounting machine guns or grenade launchers, so far, the army does not appear to have purchased them, perhaps concerned that if it is armed soldiers will take more risks with it in close combat. By comparison, earlier army unarmoured vehicles such as the jeep and Humvee were often armed.

The army plans to acquire 2,593 ISVs, enough so that each light infantry BCT can have sufficient to lift a battalion, including support elements such as mortar squads. If successful, more might be purchased for use with other types of units. The manufacturer is offering other variants such as cargo haulers and there is a test version carrying a laser for counter-UAS.

M1301 Infantry Squad Vehicle	
Produced:	2020 – present
Manufacturer:	General Motors Defense LLC
Specifications	
Crew:	Nine (one infantry squad)
Engine:	2.8l four-cylinder turbo-diesel (275hp)
Payload:	1,452kg (3,200lb)

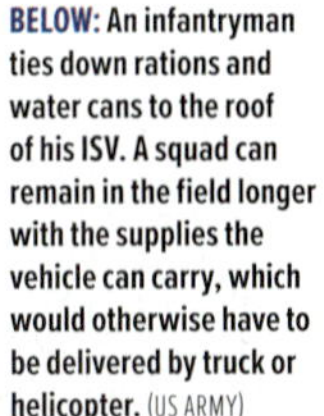

LEFT: The ISV fits inside a CH47 Chinook heavy lift helicopter but can also be carried by sling-load. (US ARMY)

BELOW: An infantryman ties down rations and water cans to the roof of his ISV. A squad can remain in the field longer with the supplies the vehicle can carry, which would otherwise have to be delivered by truck or helicopter. (US ARMY)

Armoured Multi-Purpose Vehicle

Replacing the venerable M113 series

RIGHT: A medic from the 3rd Infantry Division checks the blood pressure of a patient in the compartment of an M1284 medical evacuation vehicle. (US ARMY)

BELOW: The US Army is testing a turreted mortar system with a breech-loaded 120mm semi-automated weapon. This would allow mortar crews to fire without exposing themselves to enemy fire. (US ARMY)

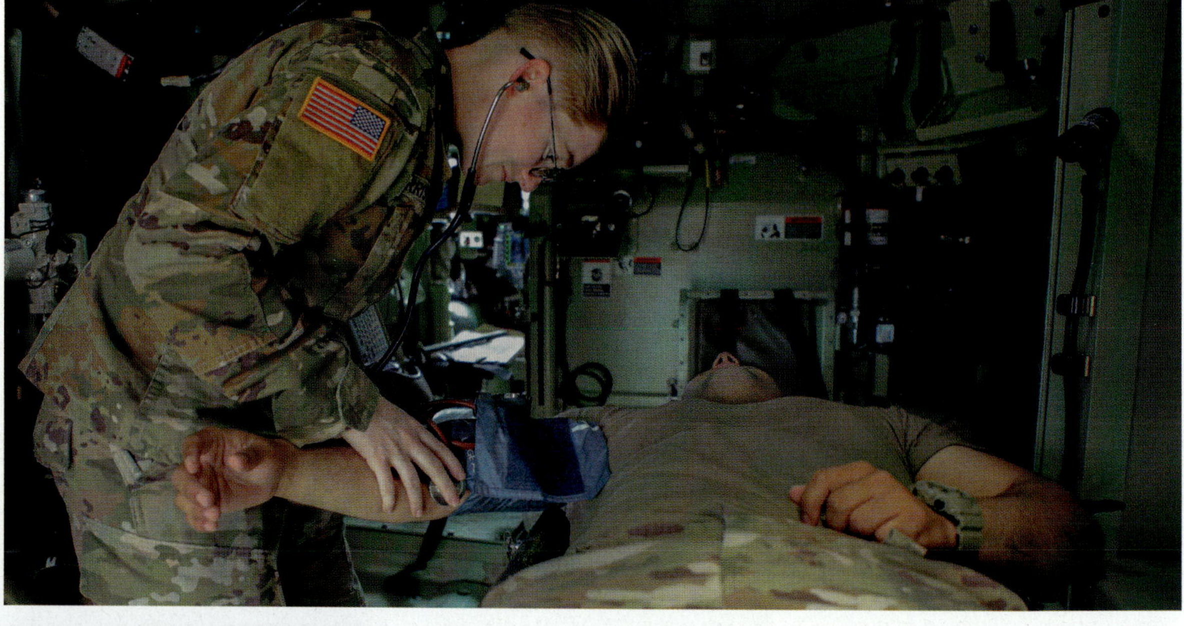

The Armoured Multi-Purpose Vehicle (AMPV) is the long-awaited replacement for the M113 series of armoured personnel carriers. The M113 was versatile and durable but had reached the end of its useful life. The army adopted the AMPV for its superior armour protection and higher speed, making it better able to keep pace with the vehicles in an armoured BCT.

The AMPV is essentially a turretless variant of the Bradley IFV, sharing its drivetrain and suspension, among other components, simplifying maintenance and parts commonality This gives it comparable cross-country performance to the Bradley and Abrams, the primary armoured vehicles in an armoured BCT. It can be fitted with armour upgrades including reactive armour blocks to increase survivability.

While the AMPV is not intended to fill the role of an IFV, it fills other roles within a BCT which still require an armoured vehicle. There are five initial variants with separate designations, including a general support version (M1283) which can fill a variety of basic roles. Other variants include a mortar carrier (M1287) for the 120mm mortar used in armoured brigades and a command vehicle (M1286) for battalion and brigade commanders and staff to lead, control and communicate with their subordinate elements. Two medical vehicles provide care for the wounded: an evacuation vehicle (M1284) to move casualties out of immediate danger and a treatment vehicle (M1285) envisioned as an 'operating room on tracks' to provide immediate life-saving care for the seriously wounded.

The manufacturer, BAE Systems, has several other variants under test, including air defence, engineer and IFV versions, the latter with a remotely operated 30mm gun turret. There is also another mortar carrier variant with an enclosed 120mm breech loading mortar turret. In 2024 BAE received $981m in contracts to produce an estimated 381 vehicles in addition to the 628 the US Army had received by 2023.

The army currently plans to buy about 3,000 AMPVs to replace about 2,900 M113s currently in BCTs. However, the service has about another 2,000 M113s in units outside the BCTs which will also need eventual replacement, possibly increasing the number the army will acquire. The US has also transferred at least 900 M113s, mostly taken from the National Guard to Ukraine which will be replaced by AMPVs over time.

Precision Strike Missile

New long-range striking power

The US Army is now in possession of the Precision Strike Missile (PrSM, nicknamed the 'Prism'). While the missile is new to service, there are sufficient quantities for field testing and training of MLRS unit members. The PrSM is replacing the current Army Tactical Missile Systems (ATACMS), which first saw combat use in the 1991 Gulf War.

The new weapon is smaller than the ATACMs, so that two PrSM missiles fit in a single MLRS ammunition pod, as opposed to one ATACMs in the same space. The PrSM is also longer ranged than the ATACMs, with the initial variant able to reach targets 500km away. This range is legally achievable since United States withdrew from the Intermediate Nuclear Forces Treaty in 2019, believing Russia had already broken it. The treaty prohibited missiles with ranges over 500km. It is unlikely the treaty will be reinstated unless China and India agree to join.

The initial variant of the PrSM, known as Increment One, has a 200lb tungsten fragmentation warhead, possibly similar to the M30A1 MLRS rocket. There are further variants under development. These versions include a multimode seeker, which allows the missile to engage moving targets.

Increment Two is the Land Based Anti-Ship Missile (LBASM). This variant will also have a longer range, believed to extend to 1,000km. This would enable attacks on targets outside the range of many opponent's own weapons systems. Future variants are believed to add new warhead types, such as a high-explosive type able to destroy underground bunkers. They will also be faster and able to engage targets on land or sea as needed. This is the US Army's first real anti-ship capability since the days of the Coastal Artillery Branch in the 1930s and 40s.

The PrSM will equip field artillery MLRS units and the Army's Multi-Domain Task Forces (MDTF), of which it plans to create five. Long-range anti-ship weapons will give these units the ability to emplace on an island in the Pacific, for example and control the waters around it for a considerable distance. In June 2024, the army tested the PrSM, striking a retired US Navy amphibious assault ship with two missiles using a National Guard HIMARS detachment attached to the 3rd MDTF (see page 28). Land targets for the PrSM would include air defence systems, headquarters elements, supply depots and other high value targets.

ABOVE: A PrSM launches from an M142 HIMARS, which can fire two such missiles before reloading. (US ARMY)

LEFT: The PrSM successfully hit a moving ship at sea during a Pacific exercise at Palau in 2024. This ship was struck during a similar exercise near Hawaii. (US ARMY)

BGM-71 TOW

Long serving anti-tank missile

ABOVE: A TOW missile emerges from the launch tube of a Stryker anti-tank vehicle during a NATO exercise in Germany.
(US ARMY)

BELOW: The backblast area of a TOW is considerable, and the flash can give away the firer's position. Crews must be ready to move quickly after shooting.
(US ARMY)

The TOW missile is the US Army's legacy anti-tank missile system and is in service with dozens of other nations around the world. TOW is an acronym standing for Tube-launched, Optically tracked, Wire guided. It can be fired from a ground mount tripod, mounted in box launchers such as on the Bradley and Stryker, or fired by aircraft such as attack helicopters.

The US Army adopted the TOW in 1970 during the Vietnam war. US forces first used it in combat in 1972 while supporting South Vietnamese forces against a North Vietnamese invasion. The missiles were mounted on UH-1 helicopters and destroyed an estimated two dozen enemy tanks.

Since then, it has seen service in almost every major conflict American forces have taken part in. Raytheon currently manufactures it, and they report over 700,000 TOW missiles have been produced through 2024.

When the missile is fired, it soft launches from the tube to gain distance from the firer before the rocket motor ignites. The weapon's control fins extend, and the rocket motor accelerates the missile to around 1,000kph before burning out, leaving the missile to glide for the remainder of its engagement time. A wire trails out behind the TOW, allowing the firer to send course corrections to the missile to keep it aimed at the target as it moves. The

missile does not arm until it is 65m from the launcher. The missile flies just over two metres above the firer's line of sight, giving them a clear view of the target.

A disadvantage of wire guidance is the possibility of the wire being cut during flight. Also, the firer must remain still while guiding the missile. If a targeted enemy spots the missile launch, they will fire at the launch point to throw off the firer's aim. However, if the firer can keep their sights on target, the TOW is accurate out to its maximum range.

Different versions of the missile have different ranges and warheads. The most common anti-tank version of TOW is the TOW 2B. It has a tandem charge warhead. This means there are two warheads, the first to detonate any reactive armour on the target and the second to penetrate its armour. The BGM-71H is designed to destroy fortifications and can penetrate up to 200mm of double reinforced concrete.

BGM-71 TOW Missile	
In service	1970
Length	1.1 to 2.5m depending on version
Diameter	15.2cm
Weight	Up to 22.6kg
Armour penetration	Up to 900mm
Range	3,750m (BGM-71F: 4,500m)

War in the Pacific

Timing is key to how the US Army will take part in a Pacific War. China aims to keep United States forces thousands of miles away from its coastline, preventing interference in Chinese goals. It is doing so through a massive buildup of naval and air power. Many onlookers assume that any war in the region will have minimal involvement of army units and assets. While it is true such a conflict will depend on naval and air power for success, land power will be needed and there are ways in which army units would enable US victory.

If there is warning of a coming war, allowing time to prepare, army forces will be prepositioned, well-supplied and placed to threaten Chinese freedom of movement. Multi-Domain Task Forces (MDTF) will be emplaced on Pacific islands where they can both dig in but also move to avoid attack. They will control the area around these islands, enabling naval and air forces to operate with less risk. MDTFs will likely get infantry as security forces, in case of a Chinese amphibious or air assault, and to guard against Chinese SOF teams landing covertly and targeting the MDTF for long range strikes.

US Army combat units would defend critical terrain and work with allies. A division in Taiwan before the Chinese can initiate an attack could deter a war from even starting. US regional allies will host combat units, allowing more army long range fires and air/missile defence units to join the fight and infantry and armour forces to bolster the local forces. This is true of well-established allies such as Japan, South Korea, and the Philippines, and potential ones such as Vietnam and India. Army logistics assets would help keep the entire military supplied.

If the war comes suddenly, the US Army will have to fight its way into range, much as it did in the island-hopping campaigns of World War Two. MDTFs will set up as close as they can in places like Guam. Once there they would have to make or seize opportunities to advance to islands and land masses closer to the combat area, slowly forcing Chinese forces back alongside the

LEFT: The 25th Infantry Division is the US Army's primary combat unit for the Pacific region. These members of the unit are on a night reconnaissance mission. (US ARMY)

navy and air force. Many predict a Pacific war would be over in weeks or months as forces and stockpiles are exhausted, but such a war could easily drag on for years. In either case, keeping army forces supplied in an environment of naval and air parity with an opponent will present challenges the US military has not faced in decades.

BELOW: A tactical truck tows a launcher for the Long-Range Hypersonic Weapon. Army MDTFs will be equipped with a battery of these new missiles. (US ARMY)

War in Europe

NATO's eastern flank

ABOVE: An infantry fire team dismounts from their M2 Bradley IFV during a live fire range event. Three of them are wearing old pattern chemical warfare suits. (US ARMY)

The risk of war between NATO and Russia is greater due to the Russian invasion of Ukraine. If Russia emerges from that war victorious (as it will likely claim no matter the outcome) it could be emboldened to invade other territories, such as the Baltic states or new NATO members Finland and Sweden, with whom it shares borders. It also shares borders with NATO nations in eastern Europe, meaning a war could spread along NATO's entire eastern edge.

A war in Europe would involve US troops on a wide scale. NATO is currently using multi-nation battle groups to train in interoperability and territorial defence. Some of these battle groups would need US Army BCTs to stiffen them and provide the modern capabilities some NATO members lack. This includes UAS, electronic warfare, and long-range fires. The current regimen of NATO exercises seems to be honing this joint warfare capability.

While some BCTs would reinforce NATO allies, it is likely the US Army would form at least one corps-sized force of its own, perhaps including units from the more capable NATO partners such as the UK or France. The US Army is offensive minded and will form a striking force to carry the fight to the Russians. The Northern European Plain spans from Germany into Russia and is good tank country.

This corps or field army would be armour heavy. While a large-scale invasion or occupation of Russian territory is unlikely, an offensive to break their ground power might easily cross the border to accomplish its mission.

Other BCTs would deploy to the forests and Arctic tundra of Sweden, Norway, and Finland. There, they would join with national troops and blunt any Russian assaults and possibly launch attacks of their own as the secondary effort in a counterattack. US forces already in Europe can be quickly reinforced by troops flown in from the United States, who can draw upon prepositioned weapons and equipment. This would allow the rapid creation of large combat formations with follow on forces from the US, including National Guard divisions, as reinforcements to maintain momentum.

Overwatching all of this would be multi-domain task forces, providing air defence, long range fires and electronic warfare support. Additional air defence battalions would defend against Russian air, missile and UAS attacks. HIMARS and MLRS battalions would launch missile strikes on critical targets like headquarters and ammunition depots. Though behind the front lines, these units would need protection from Russian special operations forces and sabotage by Russian agents.

RIGHT: Europe is heavily urbanised; soldiers will have to fight in towns and cities in a European war. These soldiers of the 2nd Armored Cavalry Brigade enter a shoot house to perfect their room-clearing skills. (US ARMY)

A Renewed Korean War

Conflict on the Korean Peninsula

Logically, North Korea should not renew the war on the Korean Peninsula. The regime's primary goal is its own survival, and war is always unpredictable in duration and outcome. While it often acts aggressive and unstable, North Korea's leadership actually acts rationally in its own way. However, wars are not entirely rational, and can be started by miscalculation or mistake, so the threat of a continuation of the Korean War remains.

The North Korean People's Army (NKPA) is a mix of capabilities. It possesses nuclear weapons and a proven cyber capability, while its conventional weapons are numerous but largely obsolete. The NKPA is one of the world's largest armies in personnel strength, but many of its troops are reportedly used for farming and construction duties, and some were recently sent to Russia for participation in the Ukraine War. Its large artillery force could rain destruction on the South Korean city of Seoul, but how long they could maintain large-scale military operation is uncertain.

In the event of a North Korea attack, the bulk of the fighting would be borne by the South Korean Army (ROK), reinforced by the US 2nd Infantry Division, which is actually a combined US/ROK unit. Brigades from the 25th Infantry

and 11th Airborne divisions could quickly move to the peninsula, as it is unlikely the NKPA air force could achieve air superiority to prevent fast airlifts. These units would be followed quickly by armoured brigades, which would need more time to deploy their heavy equipment via ship.

North Korea is also a missile threat to Japan, so US Army air/missile defence units would likely deploy there to protect the island nation. The US military, particularly the army, has extensive logistical and staging assets in Japan, which allow fast reinforcement of South Korea and other regional allies. These would

have to be protected to enable the rapid arrival of reinforcements.

A Multi-Domain Task Force would have to be positioned in South Korea, as it would have difficulty ranging all targets in the north from Japan, at least until the Precision Strike Missile achieves its projected 1,000km range. Given the doubts about NKPA endurance in a long war, if US/ROK forces could hold them, they might become exhausted as allied forces grow in size and power. There is the possibility China or Russia could resupply North Korea, though that creates a threat of widening the war as US air and naval power isolate the peninsula.

ABOVE: AH-64 Apaches hover over a South Korean hill while firing 70mm rockets. The mountainous terrain in Korea provides good cover for low-flying attack helicopters.
(US ARMY)

TOP: US Army M2A4 Bradleys and South Korean K200 IFVs during a live fire exercise at Nightmare Range, South Korea. The two armies will work closely together in the event of conflict.
(US ARMY)

War in the Persian Gulf

Iran, a mountain fortress

ABOVE: Once air supremacy is gained, raids against Iranian high value targets and critical infrastructure could quickly reduce their combat power. (US ARMY)

BELOW: Long range artillery, such as these M142 HIMARS MLRS, could quickly decimate Iranian air defences, clearing the way for aviation assets. (US ARMY)

A better solution might be a series of raids along the Iranian coast to destroy port facilities, military stores and naval forces which threaten the Persian Gulf. Special Operations Forces (SOF), helicopter-borne light infantry and Marines could quickly surge ashore from land bases or ships once air and naval supremacy are achieved. Helicopters would also allow raids farther inland, though at increased risk from portable and light anti-aircraft weapons which survive the previous air and naval strikes.

A reinforced armoured division or corps, such as III Corps, stationed in Kuwait, would provide a heavy response force in case of Iranian moves into Iraq. This force would also threaten Iran's main oil fields, located in the southwestern part of the country, though it would have to pass through Iraqi territory to do so. SOF and psychological operations units could also instigate uprisings within Iran to destabilise the ruling government. The overall goal would be to collapse Iran's government and eliminate its ability to undertake offensive warfare.

The possibility of war between the United States and Iran remains a serious scenario for the US Army. American and Iranian forces have clashed several times since 1979, and US forces are currently seeing combat with terror groups which enjoy Iranian support and weapons. Though neither nation seems eager to widen this low-level conflict, miscalculations or mistakes could lead to a major war.

Naval and air forces would figure prominently in a campaign against Iran, particularly in the early stages when the focus is on destroying Iranian air defences and offensive missile and drone capability. However, US Army units would also play an important role. Long-range artillery, air defence, and electronic warfare assets could all range southern Iran from locations in nations along the southern shore of the Persian Gulf such as Saudi Arabia and the United Arab Emirates. These sorts of units are all found in a multi-domain task force (MDTF), though it would need added artillery and air defence units to provide the needed weight of fire. The 500km range of the new Precision Strike Missile puts even more of Iran within range.

A physical invasion of Iran present difficulties. Iran is largely mountainous, providing good defensive terrain to an army which would likely fight harder and longer than that of Saddam Hussein's Iraq in 2003. An occupation would be long and costly, and the American people have little stomach for another extended conflict in the Middle East.

Examples of combat units needed
1-2 THAAD air defence batteries
2-3 Patriot surface to air missile battalions
2 SHORAD point defence air defence battalions for small UAS defence
1 Multi-Domain Task Force
3-4 HIMARS/MLRS battalions
1 light infantry division with air assault capability
1 armoured division with extra air defence, artillery, and aviation assets

The Road Ahead

LEFT: A robotic Small Multi-purpose Equipment Transport (SMET) evacuates simulated casualties during a technology testing event. (US ARMY)

The US Army's preparations for the next war will continue unabated and with intensity for the next several years. The service earnestly desires to incorporate the new facets of warfare covered in this edition. This will take time, though perhaps not as much time as feared if the army is able to institute its new methods of fast acquisition and frequent upgrades of the targeting, ISR and communications systems needed for the fast pace of modern warfare.

While this focus on preparation is new in its particular concepts, the army is always looking at what is coming and trying to be ready for it. Much of the effort devoted to transformation comes from the recognition that the US Army must modernise after two decades of mainly counterinsurgency operations, where the focus was less on brand new technology than on keeping the troops in the field equipped with the best of existing hardware. This happened after the Vietnam war and the army's efforts then resulted in a plethora of new weapons still in use today, including the Abrams, Bradley, Apache, and MLRS.

While the task seems daunting, the army's efforts are bearing fruit. The experimentation process is working and getting new tech to troops in the field allows them to add their own valuable inputs. The pace of technological advancement is fast in the 21st century; in reality everyone is trying to keep up with the latest advancements and figure out how best to employ them on the battlefield. Placing new systems in soldier's hands and letting them figure out how to best incorporate them into their warfighting mission is an effective strategy.

The army is also trying to remain flexible, as the future is not written. While the scenarios in this yearbook look at the most likely near-term opponents (China, Russia, North Korea, Iran) in the most likely situations, the crises leading to war are more often surprises. If one looks at the conflicts the United States has participated in since 1945, such as Korea, Vietnam, Grenada, Panama, the Gulf War, the Balkans, and the 9/11 attacks which led to the wars in Iraq and Afghanistan, none of them would have been predicted even a year or two before they began.

The US Army is making an intellectual break with the past and engaging in prediction, historically a very difficult thing to accomplish. However, it has three things it needs to weather whatever storm may come: professionalism, determination, and a willingness to adapt based on the situation.

BELOW: Two Hawaii National Guard UH60 Blackhawk helicopters sling load all-terrain vehicles during a readiness exercise. Guard units must be able to quickly respond to both military and civil emergencies. (US ARMY)

Acronyms and Terms

ABCT	Armored Brigade Combat Team
ACR	Armored Cavalry Regiment. These units retain a regimental title but are organised like BCTs.
ATACMS	Army Tactical Missile System, being replaced by the PrSM
AWT	Attack Weapons Team, a pair of attack helicopters working together. Sometimes called an Air Weapons Team.
BCT	Brigade Combat Team
BDE	Brigade
BN	Battalion
CAB	Combat Aviation Brigade
CAG	Combat Applications Group, commonly known as Delta Force
CATV	Cold weather All-Terrain Vehicle
CONUS	Continental United States
DIVARTY	Divisional Artillery
HIMARS	High Mobility Artillery Rocket System
HMIF	Human-Machine Integrated Formations
HQ	Headquarters
HVP	Hypervelocity Projectile
IED	Improvised Explosive Device
MAAW	Multirole Anti-Armor Anti-personnel Weapon
MLRS	Multiple Launch Rocket System
M-SHORAD	Maneuver Short-Range Air Defense System
PrSM	Precision Strike Missile, pronounced 'prism'
ROK	Republic of Korea, the acronym is often used to refer to the South Korean Army
SEP	System Enhancement Package, a set of improvements applied to armoured vehicles
SFG	Special Forces Group
SOF	Special Operations Forces
THAAD	Terminal High Altitude Area Defense, a missile defence system
UAS	Unmanned Aerial Systems

PHOTO CREDITS:
Ukrainian 254th Mechanised Brigade, US Department of Defense (DoD), US Army, US Navy, US Army, National Guard

BELOW: A HIMARS of the 18th Field Artillery Brigade fires during an exercise in Estonia. Live fire exercises during forward deployments validate the ability to do the same in combat.
(US ARMY)